chickening ~~OUT~~ IN

chickening IN

From **FEAR** to Courageous **FAITH**

8 Pillars of TRANSFORMATION

JJ Gutierrez

AMBASSADOR INTERNATIONAL
GREENVILLE, SOUTH CAROLINA & BELFAST, NORTHERN IRELAND
www.ambassador-international.com

Chickening IN

From Fear to Courageous Faith, 8 Pillars of Transformation
©2020 by JJ Gutierrez
All rights reserved

ISBN: 978-1-62020-606-5
eISBN: 978-1-62020-737-6

Cover Design and Typesetting by Hannah Nichols
eBook Conversion by Anna Riebe Raats

Unless otherwise indicated, all Scripture quotations taken from the *Life Application Study Bible, New Living Translation,* copyright © 1988, 1989, 1990, 1991, 1993, 1996 by Tyndale House Publishers, Inc., Wheaton,IL 60189. All rights reserved.

Scripture marked NIV taken from THE HOLY BIBLE, NEW INTERNATIONAL VERSION®, NIV® Copyright © 1973, 1978, 1984, 2011 by Biblica, Inc.® Used by permission. All rights reserved worldwide.

AMBASSADOR INTERNATIONAL
Emerald House
411 University Ridge, Suite B14
Greenville, SC 29601, USA
www.ambassador-international.com

AMBASSADOR BOOKS
The Mount
2 Woodstock Link
Belfast, BT6 8DD, Northern Ireland, UK
www.ambassadormedia.co.uk

The colophon is a trademark of Ambassador, a Christian publishing company.

This book is dedicated to my sweet daughter Hope, without whom *Chickening IN* would not exist. God can use anyone, young or old, to encourage and inspire others.

A special thank you to my husband, David, who supported me over the years while I healed from my broken past and discovered my true identity in Christ. I love you.

To all three of my daughters: Kayla, Courtney, and Hope. It has been my life's mission to change the legacy of brokenness that was passed down from my family because I didn't want that handed to you. This book is the "new" legacy I've worked so hard to change. It's a legacy of Christ first without whom no change would have happened. May you always walk in faith.

An additional thank you to the community of people who helped me through the years. Your love and support made a difference in my life.

To Janice, Trinity, Coach Jen, Katie, Lisa, Jen, Tam, and Evelyn.

CONTENTS

CHICKENING IN INTRODUCTION

I WANTED TO SHARE MY story with you long ago. I thought of you and the struggle you might have with fear, worry, and doubt, and my heart ached. In the depth of my soul I didn't want any woman to feel what I had felt for so many years . . . alone. Fear kept me from speaking to anyone about my inner battle with anxiety, doubt, and lack of trust in God. Though I wanted to tell you my story then, the timing wasn't right. God had a lot of work to do in my heart and mind first.

Here we are now, and it seems like a lifetime . . . forty-seven years to be exact! I've battled fear over and over again. I've stumbled and even failed many times, but God kept picking me up. Eventually, I began to learn lessons about fear and faith; lessons that are shared here in this book. God's done amazing things in my life, and He's healed parts of my heart that I thought could never be mended. It's been a long time in the making, but now my story is ready.

Chickening IN is the clever yet light-hearted phrase that God gave me to share my transformation journey. I've always been a very serious person, and I imagine that Father God wanted to lighten my heart and make me smile. And surely He did, because it was my six-year-old daughter who first told me to *Chicken IN*! **I don't know why a silly twist on a common idiom made the difference, but it did. I am convinced that words have the power to change lives, because that is exactly what *Chickening IN* did for me.**

Have you ever experienced the transforming power of a word or a phrase?

God used the words *Chickening IN* to grab my attention. They were the vehicle He used to point me back to the Bible, the place where the most life changing words can be found. Maybe you've experienced the power of a Scripture in your life—suddenly you can forgive or love when it wasn't possible before. Without the Word of God, I wouldn't be sharing my *Chickening IN* journey with you. Nor would I offer it to you to use as a tool against your fear, doubt, and anxiety. The power of *Chickening IN* lies not in the phrase, but in the truth of God's Word that it is founded upon. Knowing the truth, studying the Scriptures, and allowing God to guide and lead your *Chickening IN* journey is critical because the power belongs to God. The Bible says,

> "For the word of God is alive and powerful. It is sharper than the sharpest two-edged sword, cutting between soul and spirit, between joint and marrow. It exposes our innermost thoughts and desires" (Hebrew 4:12).

I am so thankful the power of transformation is found in God and His Word. On my own, I was doomed and maybe right now you can relate to that feeling, too. But that day—the day my daughter encouraged me to *Chicken IN*—God stopped me in my tracks long enough to pause and realize that fear was running my life. I was afraid of making a mistake, failing, and losing control; I let fear bully me around. Here I was, twenty-one years into my walk with Christ and fear was still outpacing my faith and trust in God. Oh, how desperately I wanted to boldly trust God and be a water walker with Peter, but I remained safely in my boat watching others walk on the open waters with Jesus. After hearing, "*Chicken IN* mom," I changed. I was ready to climb out of the boat because I didn't want to spend one more day trapped by fear. How about you . . . are you water walking or sightseeing? Are you stepping out of the boat or clinging tightly to the seat within the boat?

Now I am experiencing victory over fear and doubt. What once held me hostage has now taken a back seat. Courage and faith are at the forefront crowding out the fear that used to reign because *Chickening IN* is more than just a power phrase—it is a lifestyle of transformation with practical and repeatable steps. That's what this book is about: transforming fear-filled lives into courageous faith-filled lives, and the exciting news is that anyone can do it!

This is not a "quick-fix," "30 days to mental fitness," or a "one and done" and fear is gone. *Chickening IN* is a journey and process of confronting fear and taking steps of faith. It's about adopting a mindset and changing the way we think and act in response to the scary things in life. It's about examining the Scriptures and allowing God's Word to penetrate deep into the fearful, worried parts of our hearts. It takes time for the Word to grow in our hearts, and since some of our deep-seeded fears and doubts have existed for years, we can't expect them to change overnight. However, with intention, discipline, and the Holy Spirit guiding us, we can replace fear with faith and doubt with hope. I am living proof that transformation is possible for those who earnestly desire it.

Don't wait one more day in fear. Today you can start living the life you were meant to live. I will walk you through the eight pillars of the *Chickening IN* lifestyle so that you can strategically loosen the power of fear over your life in a manageable way, one step at a time. Also, I will candidly share some of my own personal stories of *Chickening IN*, chickening out, and what I have learned so that you won't feel alone. It's time to start gaining back the life that fear has tried to keep you from having.

Are you in need of a transformation? Do you desire to be a brave, bold woman of God? The next ten chapters will equip you to make the U-turn from living in fear and doubt to living courageously by walking in faith and trusting God like never before! Will you join me on this *Chickening IN* transformation journey? No longer do you need to chicken out because together we can face our giants, climb our mountains, and step out of our boats. Together, with Christ as our foundation, we can experience the amazing, adventurous life of faith God planned for us long ago. What do you say . . . will you come along with me?

The process of completely changing from a fear-filled life to courageous faith-filled life, and the special word that God used to facilitate transformation. A word that isn't just for me, but for you, too!

Chapter 1

A TRANSFORMATION JOURNEY

THIS IS MY STORY OF transformation. It is not just another positive transformation story, but one that shares secrets and principles as well as concrete action steps to help you have a transformed life as well! To be vulnerable and honest, my life could have been so many things . . . I could have been a victim of my circumstances, I could have repeated my mother's legacy of pain, brokenness, love-affairs, and multiple marriages. I could have sunk into a life-long depression feeling sorry for myself or become an angry person living with a chip on my shoulder. I had every right to be those things, but I wanted more. I had deep, desperate longings and needs for security, hope, and love. Life was brutal to me. It stole, extorted, twisted, and manipulated me. But, and I mean a huge *BUT*, God had a different plan. A transformational plan to teach me, heal me, and change me into a new person. Because of that **I have learned practical ways to face my fear, create action plans, take smart chances, and be happy with who I am.**

I am now able to travel down unknown roads with new-found boldness and have dreams again—BIG dreams! No longer controlled by fear and triggers of a painful past, I have been transformed. You, too, can have a transformed life. I am living proof of it! If it can work for me, it can work for YOU! We need hope, faith, inspiration, and forward movement to change. I call it putting feet to your faith, and this book is written to provide you with the practical steps that worked for me. In this chapter, I want to share with you the importance of forward movement, the roadblocks that prevent us from taking positive action, examples from my life, and the phrase that has guided me to transform and write this book.

Putting feet to our faith and taking action is God's way of transforming us!

The principles laid out in this book are not something I just stumbled upon or made up myself. If it were all about me, the foundation would fail because I am just a human being with faults and weaknesses. But instead, we need something or Someone greater. What better place to go than the Bible! In fact, what I want to share is that putting feet to our faith and taking action is God's way of transforming us! Let's look to the Word of God for great examples of the kind of transformation action I am talking about.

In Matthew 9:20-22, we learn about a woman who was bleeding for years. She heard Jesus was in town and she thought, "If I could just touch His robe I will be healed." She didn't let it end there with just her thoughts. Instead, she put feet to her faith by purposely seeking Him out to touch His garment. Because of her active faith, God healed her. It took intentional, courageous movement for a sickly, discouraged woman to find Jesus that day. And Jesus, not caught off guard, responded with compassion and love.

Another example is Noah, who by faith took action and built a boat—a very large boat at that! It had never rained before and he didn't live near a large body of water, so everyone thought he was crazy. But, because of his faith in God, he took action and obeyed what God told him to do. And that action saved him, his family, and the entire animal kingdom.

The Bible is full of examples of people who acted upon God's word in faith. They couldn't see the end result, but without action they were sure not to arrive at the destination. This is the key difference between the stuck and the unstuck, being trapped in a broken, discouraged life or being transformed into a new life of healing, joy, and wholeness. *The key is action.*

See, the truth is that if you want a transformed life, that life is about action and taking steps even if they are small. The Bible says that we are saved by grace not by works, yet our works show our faith (James 2:17-18). True faith is faith in action, and if I really believe that God has a better life for me, then **my actions will display my belief in God**. It is one thing to hear the word of God and get excited about it. It is an entirely different thing to hear the word of God, get excited about it, and act. Faith is not just believing—it is believing and acting upon that belief. I love what Focus on the Family says, "Faith is acting like God is telling the truth."[1] If you believe it, you will do it.

The moment you decide to take action, you may immediately be met with opposition. Satan would like nothing more than to keep me and you enslaved by fear, stuck in anxiety, and paralyzed by pain. He doesn't like faith in action. Keeping me and you immobile is his goal. For me, opposition came in the form of strongholds and ensuing negative self-talk. Satan is clever and his goal is to plant seeds of confusion. If he could get me to entertain his lies, then they had a chance to grow in my heart. It doesn't take much. I can testify that the enemy has preyed on my weaknesses as if he has studied them with a fine-tooth comb knowing exactly what to spew at me. Thankfully, I am not left defenseless. Jesus has defeated the enemy and with every lie, Jesus covers me with His love. He has the final say over my life.

It is all too easy to allow fear and lack of courage to cause us to accept a mediocre life, a life trapped by all the wild and crazy "what-if's" thrown our way. These fears might come from well-meaning family and friends or your inner self-talk. It could be the enemy of your soul, Satan himself, hurling just enough doubt to keep you from action. Whatever the source, it doesn't take much. Like yeast in bread, it takes only a little fear to bend our gaze away from God so that we forget the power of a faith-filled life.

> Like yeast in bread, it takes only a little fear to bend our gaze away from God so that we forget the power of a faith-filled life.

When I first encountered the importance of action, it took intentional attention and courage, as well as resolve against the negative self-talk, to call and schedule an appointment with a counselor that day. I wasn't sure if she would be able to help me, but I knew

I couldn't keep living the way I was living. I was exhausted from the intense anxiety and fear I was experiencing, my marriage was in a slump, and I was in a career that was draining any sense of joy from my life. My youngest daughter, a toddler at the time, had anxiety, too, and that came with many parenting challenges I didn't expect. I felt completely unequipped. My faith was being challenged as I questioned, "If I am a Christian and I believe in the power Christ, why am I living in fear and doubt? Why am I not living like I really trust God?" I needed help.

The next six to twelve months were a whirlwind for me. They were filled with confronting fears and learning to combat lies. For the first time in my life, I was forced to face my fears, my pain, and the things that fueled my anxiety. It was at times unbearable.

I shed many tears—gut wrenching tears—as I looked back at my past. Life seemed so unfair. Cancer won the battle for my mother's life and I became motherless at eighteen. But I felt motherless most of my life anyway, because she was preoccupied with love affairs, resulting in multiple marriages and divorces that had devastating effects on me and my sisters. About a year after losing my mom, I had my first daughter out of wedlock, and my pain compounded because I promised myself my kids would never experience what I had with my step-dads. Yet, here I was having a little girl on my own. A few years later, I was swept off my feet. Head over heels in love. We married quickly, and it is no surprise that the first few years were challenging. We both brought baggage—a lot of baggage. The marriage was up and down like a roller coaster. Then came separation and almost divorce. I felt so ashamed. This pain was deeper than anything I had ever experienced.

Before transformation, depression and anxiety were a normal part of my daily life. I felt embarrassed about it and hid it from most people. I had been a Christian for many years at this point, and I questioned God. How could this be happening to me? Was my faith not strong enough?

During that first counseling session, we discussed having a new life and the word *transformation* came to mind. It just kept swirling around in my head. I longed for it more than anything, but I wondered if my longings were nothing but a fairytale that would never come true. To be transformed means a marked change in appearance, character, or nature, especially for the better. I knew when I accepted Christ in my heart I was transformed from death to life. I was forgiven of my sins by the blood of Jesus and eternity was secured immediately. It was a spiritual transformation that occurred the very moment I called out to God. But while the spiritual transformation was there, the transformations of my mind and emotions were not there yet. I was still suffering from the consequences of a broken past, the uncontrollable, hurtful things that happened to me, and the bad choices I made. I will continue the story in the next chapter, but first, I want to circle back to address five specific roadblocks that held me prisoner and kept me from taking action and putting feet to my faith. Maybe you can identify with some of these?

1. FEAR

"This is my command—be strong and courageous! Do not be afraid or discouraged. For the Lord your God is with you wherever you go" (Joshua 1:9).

The Bible is full of commands about fear and for good reason: fear hinders us and can sabotage the transformation God wants to give us before we even get to taste the "promised land" of what God has to offer. In fact, it almost kept Israel from entering the actual promised land God had given them. The sad thing is that often what we fear is an exaggeration of truth or so far-fetched it's nearly impossible. In my life, I was constantly running from fears that I had no proof would ever come true. Or my "proof" was based on a limited experience, not the Word of God. Fear tried to keep me from facing the pain of my past and from embracing the hope of my future. Fear tried to keep me from every big thing I have ever done.

You can recognize fear when you have thoughts like these: *What if I fail? What if I can't do this? What if something bad happens? What if I am embarrassed? What if I am not good enough?* It is powerful and dangerous to entertain these thoughts for too long. Fear steals hope, transformation, and action if we let it! At times, fear feels like a good thing because it keeps us safe, but we really have to consider what "safety" might be costing us. Sometimes it helps to do something as simple as making a cost and benefit list to consider what fear is costing you. Maybe it costs you closeness in relationships. Maybe it costs you your dream. Maybe it costs you a lesson that you needed to learn that would be helpful for the rest of your life. Maybe it costs you a better future.

2. DOUBT

"But when you ask him, be sure that you really expect Him to answer, for a doubtful mind is as unsettled as a wave of the sea that is driven and tossed by the wind. People like that should not expect to receive anything from the Lord" (James 1:6-7).

Doubt is so powerful that when we give into it, we limit God's infinite transforming power. Take a moment to let that sink in! Doubt says that we know there is something good in God, but instead of embracing Him, we question Him. Maybe there is an underlying belief that we do not deserve it, or we do not want to face disappointment. Doubtful thinking limits what we have access to, and what we do not have access to. It is like taking a key to a room of treasure and saying you're worried the key won't fit, so you just throw the key away instead of opening the door to discover abundance.

Doubt is a doorway to depression. I have firsthand experience. There was a time when my teenage daughter was going through some very difficult life situations and I doubted whether I was a good mom or not. I knew deep in my heart I had done everything I could to love and teach my daughter but watching her suffer through pain created doubt in me. That doubt turned into thirty days of deep depression that required medical intervention. I allowed doubt to overpower what I knew was truth. Thankfully, with help I was able to overcome depression and, as Christian author and speaker Joyce Meyer puts it, "my stinking thinking!"[2] Sometimes doubt needs to be addressed head on by taking an honest analysis of your thoughts to see if you, too, have "stinking thinking."

3. WORRY

"So don't worry about tomorrow, for tomorrow will bring its own worries.
Today's trouble is enough for today" (Matthew 6:34).

While doubt invokes depression, worry creates anxiety. It is a constant swirling of thoughts much like a tornado that spirals out of control. God tells us not to worry, again, because He wants us to live a transformed and powerful life. There is nothing more debilitating than playing guessing games with what might happen by anticipating the outcomes. It wouldn't be so bad if our anticipation was for positive, happy outcomes, but nine times out of ten it is the worst-case scenario. I experience worry almost daily. I am so afraid of losing a loved one . . . maybe because of the loss of my mother at a young age. But whatever the reason, if my loved ones are late getting home or I haven't heard from them when I should have, I begin to mull over what might have happened to them. The worry gains force similar to the winds of a tornado and before you know it, I am experiencing grief and loss, and they are only a few minutes late!

Worrier's thoughts often sound like this: *What if I do something wrong? What if I make a mistake? What if this wasn't what God wanted me to do? How can I be sure this was the right decision? What if someone dies or gets sick? What if I get sick?* The worry can go on and on, and, just like a tornado, it leaves a ton of wreckage behind. I worried I would never heal from my past and that a normal life was out of reach, but thankfully God had other plans for me. And He has other plans for you, too! I have found that confessing my worry to God every moment it happens leads to a more peaceful mind. It takes discipline, but it is well worth the effort!

4. LOW SELF-ESTEEM

"The God looked over all He had made, and He saw that is was excellent in
every way. This all happened on the sixth day" (Genesis 1:31).

If we are children of God, there is no need to believe that we are not good enough or that our past mistakes define how valuable we are. Self-esteem is something that should not be based on what we think, but on what God thinks instead! Often, low self-esteem sounds like these thoughts: *I am not smart enough, pretty enough, or strong enough. If people really knew me, they would not like me.* Low self-esteem is thinking too lowly of yourself while pride is thinking too much of yourself. Healthy esteem comes from God.

The danger of low self-esteem is the inability to take any action, but it goes a little deeper into the heart than *I can't* or *I am not good enough.* It is a feeling in your core of unworthiness, shame, or uselessness. One powerful mindset to adopt is soaking in self-esteem based on what God says about us! Like a sponge absorbing in water, bathe yourself in the Word with Scriptures like this: "How precious are your thoughts about me, O God. They cannot be numbered" (Psalm 139:17)! You can have confidence to try and even fail because your self-esteem is God-based. Next time you are feeling unworthy, I encourage you to look up Scriptures and agree that God knows your worth better than you!

5. SELF-SUFFICIENCY

"As iron sharpens iron, a friend sharpens a friend" (Proverbs 27:17).

I like to define self-sufficiency as having an independent spirit. Being independent is good to a point, but never as an extreme and never at the exclusion of God and the people He has put in our lives. When you have a broken past or have experienced great emotional pain, it is natural to become emotionally independent and believe that you cannot trust others. For me, self-sufficiency created a barrier to asking for help when I needed it or connecting deeply with loved ones, including my husband. My comfort zone is at a distance. It is self-protection.

Self-sufficiency sounds like this: *I can't depend on anyone. I must do it myself. I have to take care of myself because no one else will. Don't be vulnerable and allow others to get too close. They will just disappoint me and hurt me.* The ironic thing is that vulnerability usually brings people closer together. Yes, we do have to be careful whom we trust, but not trusting anyone (including God) is ultimate separation. Trusting and allowing another person to influence you in a good way leads to life.

One way to challenge this is to practice trusting others. We trust in things around us all the time! But if we expect perfection from others, we will be disappointed.

In order to truly make progress, I have had to confront these roadblocks in my mind one by one either altogether or individually. Now, in life, I am actively confronting them, sometimes stumbling, giving up, and then trying again. But there is one phrase that has given me the strength to continue, even when I feel I cannot. **The phrase that strengthens me to fight against these five roadblocks of lies is the phrase *Chickening IN*.**

God certainly has a sense of humor because I struggle with fear daily, and it was my six-year-old daughter who gave me this phrase—a new twist on an old idiom. God was also gracious because He knew I had been struggling with a VERY BIG, life-changing decision that I had attempted to make multiple times. The kind of decision that gives your stomach butterflies, both excitement and anxiety at the same time; the kind of decision that requires a leap of faith into unknown territory. I was sitting at Panera Bread with my daughter and her tutor. I was explaining to the tutor that I was afraid of making this life-changing decision, and with a concerned tone I said, "I chickened out again!" We both giggled, knowing life decisions are difficult. From across the table, in a sudden, confident, matter-of-fact voice, my daughter said, "Chicken IN mom, just Chicken IN!"

My thoughts stopped in their tracks—I had never heard of such a thing and I had to take it in and process. Did my daughter just invent a new idiom? The tutor and I both laughed at it, but the truth was, I had spent years struggling to make this one decision. With the help of that phrase, I was able to grow feet to my faith and in one moment, a wise six year old inspired me to stop chickening out and rather to *Chicken IN* and have courage to make the decision.

Throughout my life, I was very familiar with chickening out. It is a common and widely used idiom that means to back out from fear, lose one's nerve, cowardly, or to decide not to act due to fear. Most likely you have heard or even used these phrases: you're a chicken, chickening out, or don't chicken out.

The exact opposite is true of *Chickening IN*. It means to complete or finish in the face of fear, step up to the plate of your life, follow your dreams, be courageous and bold, live in faith, travel the unknown, and take calculated risks. It

> **chickening IN means to courageously and intentionally put feet to your faith.**

means to be who God created you to be and not live life by chance, happenstance, fear, or less than you were made to be. **In the simplest terms, *Chickening IN* means to courageously and intentionally put feet to your faith.**

Chickening IN has become a way of life. It gets me to take action and to resist the five roadblocks of opposition to action. But beyond that, this phrase transforms fear and doubt into forward motion, faith, and practical application. *It takes courage to change—no, it takes GREAT courage to change.*

As I have practiced *Chickening IN*, I have realized that there are eight pillars to this principle. I created the pillars to provide practical steps to putting forward movement to faith. Trusting God and taking steps of faith has been hard. Overcome by fear and anxiety, God has worked diligently in my life to transform me from the inside out. It has never been passive. God has always required action on my part. Not because He needs me, but because He wants me to learn and grow and to understand how great His love is for me. Here are the eight pillars:

1. Facing Fear

2. Stepping Up to the Plate of Your Life

3. Taking Calculated Risks

4. Traveling the Unknown Road

5. Embracing Your Uniqueness

6. Pursuing Your Dreams

7. Doing It Afraid

8. Faith the Difference Maker

As I look at this list, I think about you and I wonder if you, too, need these pillars of support to *Chicken IN*? I think of people I have known and my heart cries for the hurting wife who feels alone in her marriage and the mother fighting with all her grit to be a great mom because her mom neglected her and left her to raise herself. I am grieved for the woman who lacks clear direction and doesn't understand her purpose in this world, and for the woman who endlessly strives for perfection only to find out it is unattainable. My heart aches at the thought of these women going one more day without knowing they can have a different life. As much as I want a better life myself, I also desire that for you.

Do you want a better, transformed life? One where you can heal from the past, face your fears, love who God made you to be and dream again? If yes, then I invite you on the journey with me. Let's stop chickening out in life and together let's step up and actively pursue the life God has prepared for us. How does restored hope, adventure, excitement, and a new life sound to you? Fantastic, right? However, I want to be honest and transparent—it isn't all bells and whistles. It will require deep thinking, self-assessing honestly, working through fears and doubts, confronting the pain that imprisons, as well as taking uncomfortable forward movement. And it is important to remember that life isn't perfect, so we are not striving for an ideal life. Rather, the goal is to move through life's challenges with courage and faith by refusing to stay stuck in hopelessness. What do you say? Don't chicken out now! Let's take the action steps and *Chicken IN* to a transformed life together!

ACTION STEPS:

1. Identify one or more things you would like to be able to *Chicken IN* to doing. (Don't worry, you don't have to do it now. Just identifying your goal is a big step of action).

2. Thinking back on the times you have chickened out, which of the five roadblocks most often get in the way of taking action?

Confronting the internal conversation with fear. Refuting the lies with truth by moving the conversation with fear to a conversation with God.

Chapter 2
PILLAR #1 - FACING FEAR

FEAR IS A COMMON AND natural emotion felt by everyone. It can be described as the anxiety caused by anticipating the outcome of a situation. It is a God-given feeling that serves the purpose of giving information that will keep us safe from harm. Fear provides an instinctual reaction to stay away or run when we are confronted with dangerous situations like a busy street, a hot stove, or a vicious dog. But fear is also experienced in less serious circumstances like giving a speech or starting a new job. Fear *can* be wise, and when the threat is real we should listen to its prompting to run, halt, or seek help. Fear's goal is self-preservation and God gave it to us for a reason—to protect us from *real* danger. However, fear is just information, and oftentimes the perceived danger or threat is faulty because it is not based on truth.

Fear is powerful. It not only affects our emotions but our physical body as well. Sweaty palms, a racing heartbeat, and a lump in the stomach are just a few. Yet the impact to the body happens regardless of the validity of the fear itself. The Mental Health Foundation states, "fear increases the blood flow to your muscles, increases your blood sugar and focuses your mind on the thing that's scaring you." Basically, fear becomes the center of your attention and that's good when what you are frightened of is real, but it becomes a big problem when what you are fearing is not founded in reality or is based on predictions.

Fear affects both our emotions and our physical body, causing us to question our sense of security and we become immediately overwhelmed. But

Addressing fear is critical because we all have it.

it doesn't stop there: it goes a step further by attacking a person's character with blows that paralyze any positive, forward movement. It might sound like this: *You're not good enough. It's your fault anyway. You are a failure. People will judge you. Nobody believes in you. It takes guts and you don't have any. Last time you tried you fell on your face. You don't have enough faith.* These vicious lies strive to keep you and me stuck in situations that we really want to change.

Let's clarify two kinds of fear: there is healthy fear and self-limiting fear. Healthy fear is based on evidence or experience that something or someone can cause you harm; it is not made up, exaggerated, or imagined. This is the fear you need to listen to; it keeps you from touching a burning stove or running across a busy street because the fear of getting hurt is reasonable and probable. Healthy fear is good and must be heeded.

On the other hand, self-limiting fear is *not* based on evidence that harm will happen but is produced in our thoughts and founded on made-up, false, or exaggerated possible outcomes. Self-limiting fear gains its strength in the imagination and it thrives on insecurities. To have a transformed life, we need to face this kind of fear because self-limiting fear restricts our ability to take positive forward action in life. Pastor Rick Warren says it best, "Fear is a self-imposed prison that will keep you from becoming what God intends for you to be."[3] Self-limiting fear seeks to keep life in a mediocre, habitual place by creating just enough doubt that the thought of risking and failing is too scary. It's a place in the heart where the fear of feeling pain denies healing and forgiveness. It robs and steals joy, freedom, and happiness. *Self-limiting fear is the fear we want to transform so we can have the life God desires for us.*

Transformation begins with an intentional decision to take positive action. **Addressing fear is critical because we all have it.** In fact, we all have a relationship with it, and how we manage it determines if we are facing it or it is facing us.

My relationship with Fear is much more chummy than I want to admit. Fear and I know each other too well. We've walked, talked, and buddied up as best friends—at times clinging to each other as if there were no one else. Time and again I have tried to break free from it, but Fear is a loyal companion, and the fear of being wrong, making a big mistake and failing has over-powered the voice of God calling me to walk by faith. Facing my fear has meant grabbing my old buddy Fear by the hand with bold confrontation with Fear throwing a fit and telling me all the reasons why I should listen, but I have to combat the lies. These lies are about my value, worth, and strength. Lies that keep me captive such as: *If I walk in faith, I might fail and have to go back. Does that mean I am a loser or a day-dreamer with too far-fetched dreams that will never come true? Or, should I stick to the known where life is predictable and safe because stepping out with courage is too much of a risk?*

The very big decision I referenced in chapter one when my daughter first told me to *Chicken IN* was a decision about my job. For quite some time, I felt a strong inclination that I needed to leave. It wasn't satisfying anymore. All the effort put into counseling to heal from life's pain was opening the door for the new life I desired. I was able to dream again. Hope for a purpose-ful, meaningful life was blossoming. However, Fear was my right-hand com-panion, and it had a lot to say about this. Fear didn't like the idea of change, and with every new, exciting idea I had, I was met with fearful reasons why I shouldn't. The internal debate was heated as Fear tried to convince me I wasn't smart enough, good enough, or brave enough. The lies sounded like this: *It's just too risky, play it safe,* or, *Why would you expose yourself to potential humiliation or embarrassment?*

During this time, an amazing opportunity presented itself, one that would transform my career and I wanted it. A job was posted for a local Christian nonprofit that encompassed everything I had imagined in a new job. A mentor of mine said it was as if God handed me exactly what I wished for: a Christ-centered organization with a focus on helping women where I could make a difference and use my skills and talents for a purposeful vocation. I decided to go for it and with prayer and my best effort I landed a job interview. The interview was wonderful. I made an immediate connection with the employer and by the end of the interview, we hugged goodbye. I have never hugged my interviewer before! Leaving that day I felt so hopeful and renewed; transformation was in motion. God was answering my prayers.

Weeks went by, then came a job offer. As I expected, the salary was less . . . only thirty percent of what I was currently making. I knew moving from a corporate job to a nonprofit meant a financial sacrifice, but I was willing to take a pay cut to have a meaningful job and make a difference. Sometimes following your heart means giving up something; it could be money like me, but it could also be time because you decide to go back to school or giving up friends that aren't healthy for you. Whatever the sacrifice is, fear is ready for battle.

Seeds of doubt were being planted as fear began speaking loudly to me. It sounded like this: *How can you justify moving to a job that you may or may not like for less money? How will you afford to pay for your daughter's tutors and who will care for her while you're at work? As it is right now, you get to work from home ninety percent of the time. You are lucky. Why would you give up the known for the unknown? Why would you leave a secure six-figure income with a company car, benefits, and a 401K?* While these were all valid questions to address, it seemed fear had the upper hand and was winning this conversation while my hope was sinking fast.

There are many reasons fear has had the upper hand in my life, from my childhood dysfunction to past mistakes to "what-ifs." My lack of confidence in who I was and how much I am loved provided ample fuel for fear to overpower my internal voice and the voice of God. Yet, I longed to leave my career to pursue God's calling for my life. But I didn't have any outward proof of what God planted in my heart. **It would require faith. And fear loves to attack faith.**

The voice of God is drowned out by Fear and can become a whisper or even silent.

Fear is persistent, and it will do everything it can to cause a person to give up hope. Fear's voice

isn't hard to discern. It lacks wisdom and is discouraging, doubtful, and de-
feating. The voice of God is drowned out by Fear and can become a whisper
or even silent. Recognizing Fear's voice versus God's voice is vital to understanding if Fear is controlling the conversation. I have heard Fear speak in
five specific ways: run, lie, panic, give up, and do nothing.

1. RUN

It is natural to want to run or escape when we are afraid. Upon the first wave
of fear, Fear is already prepared to hurl commands like: *Get away fast! It is not safe
to risk it. You might fail and failure brings shame. What will others think of you? Go
now before you embarrass yourself. You don't have what it takes to do this so run while
you still can!* Fear knows exactly what to say and how to make the impact very
personal. Fear can tailor a message to stir up the deepest insecurities in anyone.

I wanted to run away on that first day of counseling. I knew it meant facing my painful past and that was far too daunting. Fear spoke loudly, and the
desire to flee was strong. Fear tried to convince me that I didn't need to be in
that room and that I could handle this on my own. Fear was trying to isolate
me from God and from community. God was calling me to stay still and trust
Him like David when he cried, "But I am trusting you, O LORD, saying 'You
are my God!' My future is in your hands" (Psalm 31:14-15).

In Genesis 32:9-12, we meet up with Jacob twenty years after he had taken his
brother Esau's birthright and blessing. Not knowing if his brother was coming
to harm or kill him, Jacob became frantic with fear. It was a moment when running and fleeing would have been reasonable, and I am sure Fear's voice was loud
that day. However, Jacob, instead of listening to Fear decided to pause, gather his
thoughts, and pray. The Bible says, after praying, "Jacob stayed where he was for
the night, and prepared a present for Esau" (Genesis 32:13). Fear said to run, but
after pausing in prayer Jacob's faith told him to stay and to be ready to face his
brother. Next time you feel like running, first pray, and if God calls you to stay,
then stay.

2. LIE

There isn't a child alive that hasn't lied or bent the truth to avoid getting into trouble. The fear of being truthful because painful consequences await is quite a motivator for not only children but adults as well. The internal voice may sound like this: *Don't let anyone see the real you. The truth isn't good so lie to make yourself look better. Avoid rejection by being dishonest about your likes, dislikes, faith, or true self.*

Lying for fear that our innermost thoughts or emotions will be exposed isn't a new temptation. In Genesis we can read about God's promise to Abraham and Sarah that they would have a child. And, when Sarah overheard this, she chuckled and thought to herself it was a silly promise since she and Abraham were old and well beyond child-bearing years. When the Lord questioned Abraham about why Sarah laughed, Genesis 18:15 tells us that Sarah was afraid, so she denied that she had laughed. She didn't want her true feelings revealed, yet God already knew Sarah's true feelings, and He already knew she doubted His promise.

I can identify with Sarah, but for a different reason. It has taken me thirteen years to verbally state that I wanted to be a writer. Being extremely afraid that I would fail or that others would laugh at me thinking, *she really thinks she can write, she isn't talented or who does she think she is,* was just too much of an emotional risk. So I kept quiet and lied about my true desire and my dream. I kept it deep in my heart where it was safe from ridicule or destruction. But just like Sarah, God knew it was there, and finally I wanted the life God had for me—I could not continue to deny it.

3. PANIC AND WORRY

Word just came that your husband's company is conducting a massive layoff, or the doctor called after your mammogram asking you to come in for a second look. These are the crisis moments that panic and worry invoke over-anticipation. Fear causes "worst-case scenario" thoughts to run frantically through the mind. Panic and worry spout out questions like: *What if he loses his job? What if he can't find another job? What if we lose everything? What if the test result is cancer? What if it's terminal? What if I'm not strong enough to go through this? What if I fail?* The "what-ifs" go on and on with no end, eventually causing anxiety to well up in your gut leaving you a total mess.

I tried three times to quit my previous job but panic and worry relentlessly asserted their opinions. Rather than trusting God, I chickened out and didn't give notice. I over-anticipated the negative possibilities of quitting and undervalued all the positive gains. I neglected to remember that if God calls me, He provides the courage I need to step up in faith. His Word says, "I am the LORD your God, who teaches you what is good and leads you along the paths you should follow" (Isaiah 48:17). But not only did I listen to the worry and panic, but I obeyed it.

Under the precise circumstances, we are all prone to panic and worry and if Moses, the man appointed by God to bring the Israelites out of slavery, is susceptible to it, then we all are. In Exodus 3 and 4, God appears to Moses in a burning bush, and He gives Moses His plan on how to rescue the Israelites from the Egyptians where they had been held captive for years. In Exodus 4:1 the Bible says that Moses protested again, "Look they won't believe me! They won't do what I tell them. They'll just say, 'The Lord never appeared to you.'" Moses' fear caused him to over anticipate how the Israelites would react to the news of God's deliverance. Often, like Moses, we can build up situations in our minds and worry about everything that could go wrong instead of trusting God to provide courage, strength, and the support we need. It's easy to jump into a fearful panic. Instead, remembering that God is greater than any circumstance, we can focus on His abilities, not our fear-filled anticipation and what-ifs.

4. GIVE UP

The internal conversation with giving up might go like this: *I've tried but I haven't seen any fruit. I'm tired and I'm worn out, maybe it's time to call it quits.*

What's the point in continuing? It is a waste of time and energy. Was this really God's plan? It's too hard. Turn back now while it is not too late. Cut your losses.

I find the temptation to give up comes after taking a big risk or after the honeymoon effect has worn off, and I'm knee deep in the new situation. The excitement of *Chickening IN* has worn off and the true work has begun, but the finish line is too far out to see. It is in the middle that fear starts whispering, *Give up! You can't do this. It's too much!*

This reminds me of a familiar story in the Bible. In Matthew 14, Jesus miraculously feeds 5,000 people with five loaves of bread and two fishes. He tells His disciples to get in the boat and go to the other side of the lake. The Bible says, "Meanwhile, the disciples were in trouble far away from land, for a strong wind had risen, and they were fighting heavy waves" (Matthew 14:24). In the middle of the lake with no view of land, they were terrified. Yet, they were completely in God's will, for He had sent them on the journey. I am sure they wanted to give up, turn around, and go back. Oh, how often I find myself in that situation! When things are difficult it is easy to assume it isn't God's will, and fear will try to convince me to give up. But God is with us. Giving up seems like a good solution but rather than turning back, it's time to press deeper into our faith. God hears us in the middle and God heard the disciples, too, for the very next verse says Jesus came walking on water. No matter how afraid, worried, or tempted we are to give up, God will meet us there. He is with us, He will never forsake us, and He has the power to walk right over our circumstances.

5. DO NOTHING

Getting started is sometimes the most frightening part of making forward movement in life. Fourteen years ago when I first realized I needed major emotional healing from my past, the road ahead looked long and complicated. There wasn't one easy answer to the anxiety and depression I felt, but rather many factors that contributed to it. I was afraid it would be too much—the size of the task ahead frightened me. Fear tried to paralyze me by telling me things like: *Why try? Is healing worth the pain you have to go through to get to the other side? It is just too big to confront. You're better off leaving it alone and moving on.* Fear wanted to immobilize me.

Being afraid of the size of a job, the amount of work required, or the risk involved can cause us to do nothing. In 1 Chronicles 28, we see David encouraging his son Solomon not to fear the work of being a king. He says, "Be strong and courageous, and do the work. Don't be afraid or discouraged, for the LORD God, my God, is with you. He will not fail you or forsake you. He will see to it that all the work related to the Temple of the Lord is finished correctly" (1 Chronicles 28:20). Such powerful words direct the focus back to God. Rather than fixating on the enormity of what needs to be done, we can start chipping away by working. Basically, we need to simply get to work.

Fear will say: *Don't do anything. The work is too much. There is too much risk, just remain. Let someone else do it. They are more talented than you, more brave and more courageous. There is safety in doing nothing.* But God asks us to take a step, make progress, and do the work. Proverbs 12:11 says, "Hard work means prosperity." Prosperity isn't just financial, but could be restored relationships, healed addictions, or following the calling God has on your life.

Every person on earth feels fear, has a relationship with fear, and endures obstacles to overcome fear. For me, fear has been a stronghold and by recognizing these obstacles it has given valuable insight to overcoming and facing my fear. Some say that knowledge is power, and it is so true. Learning to identify the urge to run, give up, or panic is empowering and freeing. But identifying the obstacles is just the first step to truly *Chicken IN* and face fear. To make the process complete, we must honestly inspect the internal conversations that are happening when we want to run, lie, freeze, or do nothing.

My internal conversation with fear and this wonderful job opportunity was a roller coaster of emotion. I felt excitement at first and then anxiety as

I contemplated taking the job. Debating fear is tricky and on this occasion, I was doing my best to win. I was telling fear I needed this change and that my heart was longing to make a difference. I felt like God had provide this opportunity and I wanted to follow God, to trust Him. But fear was relentless, and it reminded me that there were so many unknowns. What would life be like with less income? How will this impact my daughter? Will this really be the answer to longings in my heart? Fear kept asking me, *What if you are wrong and you make a huge mistake?*

In the end I listened and obeyed fear, and it won. I didn't face my fear that day. I turned the job offer down. That was a few years ago and I still wrestle with *what if.* I wish I had faced my fear and that I was writing to say how brave I was and how trusting in God transformed my work and made my dreams come true. I truly regret not *Chickening IN,* not facing my fear, and not taking the job. I will always wonder what kind of impact I could have made in those women's lives had I taken the job.

I don't want you to experience the same regret I did. Please don't make my mistake by taking on fear alone. Trying to fight fear with my own voice was a losing battle. If you have ever tried, then you know it is a difficult task because fear is powerful. Fear's character attack is personal. It counts on using past mistakes, weaknesses, and pain to keep a person in bondage.

The biggest problem with fear is that it is not built on faith, but on doubt, panic, and distress. Fear exaggerates the negative and underestimates our ability and God's power. The more you engage in conversations with fear, the less success you will have over obstacles. Christian pastor and author Max Lucado states in his book *Fearless,* "It sucks the life out of the soul, curls us into an embryonic state, and drains us dry of contentment," and he points out, "no one is immune to fear."[4]

Fear wants to lead the conversation by encouraging the instinct to run, lie, panic, worry, give up, or freeze. Instead of entertaining every fearful thought that comes to mind, I have had to learn to combat those deceptive thoughts with truth. On my own, I have found minimal success. It's like shooting in the dark; occasionally I can overcome fear's demands, but transformation requires more odds than shooting in the dark and victory over fear greatly increases when I talk to God about my fear.

There are numerous stories in the Bible about people having honest conversations with God, and then, trusting God in the face of scary or impossible situations. And when they turned to God in their weakness, their strength was multiplied. In Jeremiah 1, we see Jeremiah having a conversation with God about God's call on Jeremiah's life to be a spokesperson to the world. Jeremiah was afraid and concerned, BUT he continued to have the conversation with God about his fear exclaiming, "I can't speak for you! I am too young" (Jeremiah 1:6)! It was through coming clean with God about his fear that God encouraged and strengthened Jeremiah with His promise to be with Jeremiah and to take care of him. Rather than listening to his fear, God told Jeremiah to rise up, that God would be there with him every step of the way.

Then we see Daniel who found himself in a very difficult situation that would scare anyone. The king passed a law ordering that whoever prays to anything other than the king will be thrown into the lion's den. Daniel had to make a choice: serve God or serve the king. If he chose God, he would be fed to the lions, but if he prayed to the king, he would turn his back on God and deny Him. Daniel continued his longstanding relationship with God by praying to Him three times a day, and God rewarded Daniel with great wisdom and favor in a pagan land.

If this were me, I would be shaking in my boots mulling over how painful it would feel to be eaten by a lion. But Daniel boldly faced this terrifying situation by going home and with his windows wide open, he prayed to God as he always had done. We don't know exactly what Daniel talked about with God that day, but Daniel's actions are evidence that his conversations with God gave him strength for any situation he faced. Daniel trusted God by facing the situation head-on, knowing that God is bigger and greater than anything that could come against him. His faith in action opened the door for God's deliverance. And delivered he was! Daniel was thrown into the lions' den, but the next day when the king came to check on him, Daniel walked out of the lions' den without a single scratch (Daniel 6:6-23).

Finally, in Judges 6:11-40, Gideon had an ongoing conversation with an angel of the Lord who was delivering a message to Gideon. The angel commissioned Gideon to rescue the Israelites from the Midianites. Gideon began questioning the angel and expressed his concerns that they were the weakest tribe, and that he himself was the lowliest in his family—how could God be calling him? Again, here we see an example of having an honest conversation with God about inner fears. The back-and-forth conversation continued and led to Gideon asking for signs to prove that this message was really from God. The Lord patiently answered Gideon until Gideon realized that God was with him, calling him to be strong and brave and bring the Israelites home.

Jeremiah, Daniel, and Gideon are just three examples of average people in the Bible who acted in faith, and by doing so, impossible situations were made possible. Hebrews 11 is known as the Faith Hall of Fame, and here is what is said about the faith warriors listed there: "By faith these people overthrew kingdoms, ruled with justice, and received what God had promised them. They shut the mouths of lions, quenched the flames of fire, and escaped death by the edge of the sword. Their weakness was turned to strength. They became strong in the battle and put the whole armies to flight" (Hebrews 11:33-34).

> **Moving the conversation to God about your fear changes everything.**

Moving the conversation to God about your fear changes everything. Being honest before God about how you feel and coming clean is essential to transformation. From all of our Biblical examples, we can see the difference it makes when God is at the center—there is power to overcome, power to face fear, and power to have victory over our deepest concerns. *Let us increase Christ so He can decrease our fear!*

Like me, you can probably categorize people in your life into groups by those who have a positive, negative, or neutral impact on you. If you mingle with the negative people too much they begin to rub off on you. However, if you spend more time with positive and encouraging people, you will be uplifted and negative people won't have quite the same affect, in fact, they become neutral. To face fear, we need to neutralize fear by increasing our faith. To accomplish this, we need to tip the scales of the internal conversation with fear in favor of internal conversations with God. By talking more with God our faith grows. When our faith grows it moves God to act our behalf, it unlocks His promises, and it opens the door for miracles. Faith will calm you in a storm and give you strength to keep going in tough times.

When fear tells you *you can't*, faith says *but with God you can.*

Fear tells you to . . .	Faith in God tells you to . . .
Run or Flee.	Stay. Face your fear. Know God is with you.
Lie or cheat.	Always stand in truth.
Panic or worry.	Remain calm and steadfast in God's promises.
Do nothing.	Move forward, pray, and take action.
Cower or give up.	Rise up in the strength of the Lord. Refuse to quit.

Faith in God changes the internal conversation with fear. It moves you from victim of fear to victor over fear. It takes your eyes off the situation and directs your focus to God. When I refuse to let fear lead and instead put faith in God first, I experience freedom and excitement. Anxiety and hopelessness fade into the background and optimism is at the forefront. Fear may never go away completely, but it can take a backseat to your faith and hope, and in that, there is life.

Though I listened to fear and did not take the wonderful job I really wanted, fear didn't have the final say. I continued to talk to God about my need for change and my fear. God planted a new seed in my heart, which became another opportunity to face my fear and walk in faith. God is a God of second chances, and with every closed door (even the ones I close), He opens a new one. The new door was quitting my job, homeschooling my daughter (another *Chickening IN* moment that I will share later in the book), and starting a blog. I'd always wanted to write but was too afraid, and it was time to face my writing fear. This is where we catch up with the moment in Panera Bread when my daughter told me to *Chicken IN*. After three "gut-wrenching" attempts to resign, I finally gave notice, and rather than listening to fear I listened to God. I put feet to my faith.

Transformation was in motion because I faced what I feared most by talking with God and by not listening to my fear. I quit my job and began moving towards my dream of writing. But it was more than that, I was embarking on a homeschooling journey I never imagined—me, a homeschool mom? Change was happening in many areas at once. This is where the rubber meets the road—would I be successful and find purpose and meaning or would I fall flat on my face? Either way I felt liberated and excited about the future. Christian pastor, speaker, and author John Ortberg says in one of my favorite books, *All the Places to Go . . . How Will You Know?*, that, "God's primary will for your life is not the achievements you accrue; it's the person you become."[5] By taking this chance, having the fear conversation with God, and trusting Him, I was becoming a new person. Transformation was budding and hope returned. I felt alive. Fear was still present but this time it wasn't leading—God was.

I want to see *you* face your fear. That is why I am writing to you. I have led a fearful, anxious life, and I was ashamed to tell anyone. But I have learned that there is no shame with God. God is not some mysterious higher power far up in the sky pointing His finger down in disappointment. He is a kind, wonderful, and caring Father who is longing for a relationship with you and me. We can embark on this transformation journey knowing God is on our side, and though we will never do it perfectly, we will experience a better, more fulfilled life here on earth.

You, too, can face your fear by changing the inner conversation with fear to a conversation with God. It will take some practice and intentional thought, but you can do it. This is a foundational step to transforming a life filled with fear, anxiety, and doubt. It is a stepping-stone process and a journey that each of us must decide to take on our own, but we are not alone. With every movement forward, God is there with you and me. His plan is to draw us deeper into relationship with and reliance upon Him. Then, when we abandon our fears and walk in faith, we can really be amazed by His power at work in our lives. Remember that every faith step we take, it is always about God—His power, His glory, His plan—and when we face our fears we make room to see Him do amazing things in our lives!

ACTION STEPS:

1. Consider a current situation in which you are afraid to take action. What is fear telling you? Who is leading the conversation: fear or faith?

2. When you are afraid which obstacle do you struggle with most—running and fleeing, lying or bending the truth, panic and worry, freezing and doing nothing, or giving up and cowering? What can you do instead?

3. What hope does Hebrews 11:33-34 give you today?

Rising to the challenge, taking initiative, and assuming responsibility. Refusing to give up. Being the solution. Going when God calls. Action.

Chapter 3

PILLAR #2 - STEPPING UP TO THE PLATE OF YOUR LIFE

LET'S FACE IT, DIFFICULT SITUATIONS are inevitable. We cannot escape challenging and difficult times, it is part of the human journey. The difference between a transformed life and a mediocre life, or worse, a life of regret, is not the removal of troubles but a stepping up in the time of troubles. It is a very small decision that often takes enormous courage and faith. It is a bold choice to be an active participant in life. If stepping-up was easy, I wouldn't be here writing about it, but we can learn to defeat the challenges that prevent such courageous action and that will lead us to an active, faith-filled life. With God on our side and some practical application, we can have the courage we need to step up to the plate of our lives.

Action is at the core of the *Chickening IN* pillars and stepping up to the plate is no exception. Change happens with action. Not just any action but rather intentional, purposeful movement in response to life's challenges. Some of our difficulties are self-induced consequences due to making poor decisions—we've all been there—while other hard times seem to suddenly fall on us without any doing of our own. But in both situations we have equal opportunity to choose our response. How we choose to react is our responsibility and will determine if we move towards a better life or stay stuck. Let's spend a little time vetting out what stepping up means, then I will share the excuses that have prevented me from taking action and how I am learning to overcome them.

When I think of stepping up, an immediate visual of a baseball player taking his turn at bat comes to mind. While I am not a baseball fanatic, I certainly enjoy a family fun day at the local field. The entertainment is exciting with music, the dancing mascot, and the sound of the cheering crowd. Though I rarely eat hot dogs, I cannot seem to resist one at the ballpark! But what's most impressive are the players who are there to win the game. As I watch the batter walk up to the plate to prepare to bat, I can't help but wonder what is going on in his mind. The batting order is prearranged and the batters have no control over what the state-of-the-field is. The pressure to perform is there. He could be walking up to the bases loaded in the ninth inning and the game tied. Or empty bases, two outs and a pitcher who is on fire. Maybe the team is losing or the crowd's energy is low and he has to hold his head high. Whatever the situation, the batter must step up to the plate.

In baseball, the batter doesn't have a choice—he must step up to the plate. It is his job and his team is depending on him. But in life, you and I have a choice. The challenges and struggles we face might be out of our control. In fact, most of the time the greatest difficulties are those uncontrollable circumstances like a terminal diagnosis, sudden death of a loved one, loss of a job, an unexpected pregnancy, or a child gone astray. The choice is ours: step up to the plate of life or give up. While we all have endured many situations like this, there is one in particular that comes to my mind—the day my mother died.

I had so many plans as most new high school graduates do, but life was rudely interrupted by a terminal cancer diagnosis. That day, February 10, 1990, at 8:00 p.m., her nine-month-long battle with cancer ended and I stared at my mother's lifeless body. It just didn't seem real, and I was in shock. I had never experienced the death of a loved one, and as I continued to stare at her, I began to reflect. From as far back as I could remember I longed for a better life, in fact I dreamt of making my adulthood better than my childhood. As a young girl, my heart knew the lifestyle my siblings and I grew up in wasn't good and the lack parental guidance left us feeling empty, alone, and directionless. And though my mother didn't have many motherly qualities, I still loved her and losing her was devastating.

My mother had endured two surgeries, chemotherapy, and she had tried clean eating, but it wasn't enough to heal the cancer. I continued to stare at her lifeless body with anger, grief, and confusion. Why did this happen? The first eighteen years of my dysfunctional family life ended in her death. I didn't get the chance to ask her the many questions that lingered in my mind: *Why did you marry so many times? What were you searching so desperately for? Why weren't my sisters and I enough?*

A nun came into my mother's hospital room to pray with us. A few tears ran down my face. Mom was gone. She looked so lifeless and the texture of her skin seemed almost fake. Her cancer-beaten body gave-up. Still in disbelief, I bowed my head and prayed with the nun. The fear of losing my mother was realized that day. At eighteen years old, I was the oldest and the responsibility of what would come next fell upon me.

The time came to say goodbye and I left the hospital. When I got home I walked through the front door of the house I had lived in since I was five, the home I shared with my mother, two sisters, and the coming and going of men in my mother's life. The reality hit that mom was never coming back. The mail was piled high and as I dug through it, I panicked. The house was going into foreclosure and the electric company sent a final notice. The medical bills were numerous. My mother hadn't worked in months and there was no money for bills or food. My mother's fifth husband had abandoned us about a month prior, but he didn't add any value to the family anyway. I had two younger sisters under sixteen, with the youngest entrusted into my care. What was I going to do?

Many us face moments like this—times when what life has dished out is so difficult that the temptation to give up is strong. An affair, the loss of a job, enormous financial pressures, or a sudden tragedy—there is a choice

Difficult situations will happen. Situations we may or may not have control over, but how we respond is always within our control.

to make. A *Chickening IN* moment to step up or give up. Stepping up is hard. It means rising to the challenge, taking initiative, and assuming responsibility. It means moving into the offensive position and grabbing the circumstances in life and facing them head-on. For those who struggle with depression, it means getting out of bed; for the struggling marriage, it means making the call to schedule a counseling appointment; for the lonely person, it means taking initiative to meet new friends; for the financially strapped family, it means adopting a new budget, cutting costs, or getting a new job.

Difficult situations will happen. Situations we may or may not have control over, but how we respond is always within our control. It begins with one step: stepping up to the plate of life that each of us must decide to take. If you are like me, examples and visuals are helpful. The Parable of the Man with an Old Mule, an old anonymous parable, helped me understand what stepping up means. A mule was stuck in a hole with no way out. The farmer who owned the mule decided to bury him to put him out of his misery. With each shovel of dirt thrown upon the mule, instead of accepting his fate, the mule shook the dirt off. He then figured out that he could make a step with the dirt he shook off his back. Eventually dirt was shoveled upon him and shook off so many times that the mule was able to build a dirt stairway to climb out of the hole. The situation happened and it was unfortunate, but the mule had a choice to give up and die or step up and live. It was a transformational decision because he literally stepped up right out of the hole and saved his life.

There are many times when we can feel stuck in the holes of life, trapped by our circumstances or our view of them. It is a miserable and painful place to be because there seems to be no way out. It is in moments like these I turn to God's Word for wisdom and direction. In particular, on that day I was at church learning about a story I had heard many times before, but this time it had deeper meaning. I felt God speaking to my heart and showing me where and why I was stuck. God really does use the stories of the Bible to transform lives—I know it firsthand because it happens to me. And that day, God lovingly used John 5:1-9, a story of a disabled man, to reveal truth about my passivity and why I don't step up.

The Bible tells us the disabled man had been ill for thirty-eight years. All he needed to do was get into the pool to be healed but he couldn't. Instead, he watched others get into the pool and receive healing. At this particular healing pool, only one person could receive healing per day. To break it down, this man had 13,870 opportunities or 13,870 days over a thirty-eight--year period to step up to the plate of his life and get into the pool to be healed, but he didn't do it. As I listened to my pastor speak, I began to identify with the disabled man not because I am physically disabled, but because I have been crippled by fear, anxiety, doubt, and past circumstances. And like me, this man was stuck. Not only stuck by his physical disability, but by his attitude—he had let the situation overcome his hope.

As I thought about the story, I wanted to know the reasons why he didn't find a way. Why didn't he make it his daily mission to pursue getting into the pool? It seems like an extremely long time to lay near a pool that could have healed this man's condition in an instant. Transformation was literally in his sight. It's easy to judge this man and think, *I would never do that!* Yet, when I honestly reflect on my life there are situations in which I refused to step up, and I was reminded of the many years I spent in misery at a job that didn't bring purpose and meaning to my life. I could have made a change. I live in the United States and I have free choice, but just like this man, I didn't take hold of what was within arm's reach. God was using this sermon to teach me the reasons why and the practical ways I could move into action.

I continued to listen to my pastor. The Scriptures tell us another stepping up moment was happening for this man, but this time it was Jesus. Jesus came to him and asked, "Do you want to be healed?" His reply: "I can't, sir, for I have no one to put me into the pool when the water bubbles up. Someone else always gets there ahead of me" (John 5:6-7). All this man needed to say was yes. Yet, he replied with an excuse because his hopelessness turned into a lifestyle, a way of thinking that prevented him from seeking a solution and ultimately having a transformed life.

Then, I had an epiphany: just like this disabled man, excuses were preventing me from stepping up. I was undermining my own self because I was the master of excuses and these excuses resided in my mind. It was clear that my thoughts were leading to indecision and that was the foundation of staying stuck. The battle to step up to the plate of my life and overcome my passivity would have to begin with confronting the many excuses that were preventing me from moving forward with boldness and faith.

Excuses are an internal reason we create to defend our behavior. It is the refusal to act or take responsibility. Excuses provide us with a vehicle to place blame for not doing what we should, and they help to cover up underlying fears like *I am too afraid to step up or I don't want to do the work*. Sometimes our identity becomes rooted in the circumstance that needs to change and that makes change even more difficult. For the man laying by the pool, his disability was all he knew. He was used to being stuck, and when asked by Jesus if he wanted to be healed, he replied with an excuse. Excuses come so natural to mankind that we can even look back to the Garden with Adam and Eve. In Genesis 3:12-13, when God asked Adam if he had eaten the forbidden fruit he blamed Eve, and when God asked Eve she blamed the serpent.

Excuses can hinder us from making forward movement and limit our future. There are many kinds of excuses and most are founded in fear, like fear of failure, change, or the unknown just to name a few. In my job, I was the master of excuses. I was afraid of change, I lacked direction, and I felt safe staying in my comfort zone, so I came up with every reason not to step up and take responsibility for my happiness. And as I continued to listen to my pastor speaking about excuses, I was able to identify four excuses that were holding me back: the timing isn't right, it's too hard, it's not my fault, and God isn't working on my behalf.

TIMING ISN'T RIGHT

Have you ever heard the old saying "timing is everything?" While there is so much wisdom and truth in that saying, it can also become a crutch. I think of my unhappy job situation or pursuing my dream of writing where the saying "timing is everything" morphed into "timing must be perfect." Whether it be more money in the bank, the ideal job to transition to, or waiting for the busyness of life to settle down, I wanted all the stars to align for the perfect moment of transition. If you have ever tried to strive for perfection then you already realize the corner I was putting myself in, because nothing is ever perfect! Timing became an excuse I could hide behind rather than facing it courageously.

I think of the woman afraid to pursue her life-long dream to start her own business or the emotionally drained mother needing to take better care of herself. Timing becomes the issue with thoughts like: *Later when things settle down or we are more established, then I can. When the kids get older I will have time. The timing just isn't right yet . . . I'm too young, too old, or too busy.* In the Bible story about the disabled man by the pool, Jesus told the man, "Stand up, pick up your sleeping mat, and walk!" The man obeyed and he was healed! But the Jewish leaders weren't happy, and they said, "It is the Sabbath; the law forbids you to carry your mat" (John 5:10, NIV). Just think for a moment—what if the disabled man was too concerned about timing like the Jewish leaders and rather than obeying Jesus he said, "I can't be healed today because the timing is wrong. What about tomorrow?" He would have missed the most life-changing, faith-building, transformative moment God was offering him. I wonder how many times I forfeited experiencing transformative moments due to timing!

Truth be told, we all desire perfect timing, but is there really such a thing? The Bible says in Ecclesiastes, if you wait for perfect conditions, you will never get anything done. It never seemed like there was a right time to change my job, write a book, homeschool my daughter, go

> The most important things in life are usually happening at the most inconvenient times.

to counseling, or forgive my mother, and I have learned the hard way that timing is never exactly right for anything worthy of pursuit. In fact, the most important things in life are usually happening at the most inconvenient times. To experience a transformed life, we've got to get over perfection in circumstances and lay this excuse at the feet of Jesus. We need to allow Jesus to propel us into faith-filled action by renewing our minds with truth. And the truth is, perfection does not exist this side of heaven. Making peace with this reality will free us to take leaps of faith. Of course, wisdom, discernment, preparation, and counsel is advised, but when all is exhausted and you're left with the decision to move forward or stay put, this is where our faith shines. We can step up, trust God, and believe in His timing for our lives.

IT'S TOO HARD

Oh, how many times I have looked ahead at the mountain in front of me and lamented to myself, "It's just too much work, too complicated, too hard." Changing jobs or addressing my painful past meant putting a plan together that required making tough decisions and lots of work. My effort didn't come with guarantees but came with risk. So instead, discouragement and helplessness ushered me into remaining in a mediocre or unhappy situation that I reasoned was easier for me. By default, I became a bystander of my own life, passively watching my life go by because stepping up was too overwhelming and too hard.

You, too, may be facing very difficult situations that leave you feeling helpless. The road to healing from anxiety, broken relationships, or consequences of past bad choices is very complicated and there isn't one simple answer. It's in the realization of the enormity of the situation that the temptation to say, "it's too hard" is the strongest. Again, let's look at the man by the pool who sat for thirty-eight years watching others step up and be healed. He watched passively while others' lives were transformed. Though healing was a few steps away, it was too hard—too complicated—for him to get into the pool, and his discouragement turned into thirty-eight years of helplessness.

Sister, I don't want this for you or for me. *Chickening IN* is hard work because life is full of difficult decisions. No one gets a pass from God on journeying through life's toughest moments. The character God is developing in you and me is refined through the work of making tough decisions, acting in faith, and trusting God with the outcome. There is no escaping it. However, we can find strength in the Lord, even when we feel small.

In 1 Samuel 17:32-51, we read about David taking action when no one else would. As just a mere shepherd boy, he boldly stepped up to Goliath, the giant warrior who was pit against the Israelites. If Goliath won, then the Israelis would become slaves to Goliath's people, the Philistines. However, if David won, then the Philistines would become slaves to the Israelites. David grabbed five smooth stones and a sling shot and stepped out to defeat Goliath—talk about small versus large! But what David had, that I am often lacking, was the right perspective. David knew he was not alone and he was able to see the situation from God's perspective—a situation that looked impossible to everyone else was not impossible for Him. As David approached Goliath he shouted, "You come to me with sword, spear, and javelin, but I come to you in the name of the LORD of Heaven's Armies—the God of the armies of Israel, whom you have defied. Today the LORD will conquer you" (1 Samuel 17:45-46).

Today, let's start viewing our mountains and giants from God's perspective. The situation might seem impossible and too hard, but with God at the center we can find the courage and strength to move forward. Like David with his small stones, we can start with small steps; even a single baby step of faith in the right direction can make a huge difference. By shifting our gaze from the monstrous task ahead to our loving Father, we can begin to see more clearly, and in the clarity we can find small stones to help us climb. God can and does move mountains. God can and does conquer giants. The question is, are we willing to step up, do the work, take action, and trust Him when it's too hard?

IT'S NOT MY FAULT

Sometimes we are in difficult situations due to someone else's careless behavior or sin. Other times, it may simply be because of the broken world we live in. We didn't do anything to contribute to the situation, and yet we find ourselves needing to step up and be responsible. Times like these can make us angry and we can become hyper-focused on how unfair it is. We end up in a predicament that wasn't planned, and we are faced with stepping up or standing with arms folded in anger refusing to be the solution.

An example of this stubbornness is in the book of Jonah. God called him to step up and go to Nineveh to announce God's judgement on the city. The Bible says, "But Jonah got up and went in the opposite direction to get away from the Lord" (Jonah 1:3). Jonah was angry; he knew how wicked and sinful the people of Nineveh were, and Jonah didn't want to give them an opportunity to repent so he decided to turn away from God. He actually thought he could hide from God. Jonah ends up in a whale's mouth before he finally realizes he cannot run away from God. He has to let go of his anger and step up.

It is tempting to belittle Jonah's actions by thinking we would never disobey and run away from God, but I am guilty of doing this very same thing. God calls us to help those who don't deserve it, give something away that we really want to keep, or to forgive those who have offended us, and how often have we said no? Once I arrived home after leaving my mother's hospital room to find the financial mess, I could have easily walked away in anger.

Not only did my mother just die, but she left behind chaos that needed to be cleaned up by someone and I seemed to be the only one. I lost my college plans, a time of my life I would never get back. Anger could have consumed my life and caused me not to step up and be the solution. It wasn't fair, but still I had a choice to make.

I hear you, Sister. It's not fair when God is calling us to step up and be the bigger person. But God doesn't approach us with fairness so why would we expect fairness in our lives? I see it all the time with my kids as they demand the chores be divided up fairly or the piece of cake to be cut exactly in half, or in the workplace when coworkers gripe about expectations of the job claiming, "it's unfair, the expectations are too high!" If God dealt with us fairly, we would never survive a day in His holy presence. In fairness, our sin would separate us from God forever, but instead, God comes to us with love, justice, and Christ Jesus! Jesus stepped up for us. He became our solution and He redeemed us.

Sister, when God is calling you to step up when it's not your fault or it seems so unfair, remember what Christ did for you, and that you have the opportunity to be a solution. In those moments when you are caring for the neighbor's kids because their parents are off satisfying their selfish desires, or you are the only sibling willing to look after your elderly parents, or your husband left you for a younger woman and you have to raise three kids on your own, don't let anger and lack of fairness steal the opportunity God is laying before you to step up and make a difference. Life will never be fair, and when we accept it we can be free to step up. Free to push through the excuse "it's not my fault" and become part of the solution.

DISBELIEF THAT GOD IS AT WORK IN MY LIFE

There are countless times I've professed faith and trust in God, yet my actions didn't match my words. I wanted to move forward and step up but didn't. I had to ask myself this very important question and give the most honest answer I could, "Do I really believe Jesus is working in my life?" If the answer is yes, then what evidence is there? Truthfully, I didn't want to answer that question. It was too painful because I considered myself a strong Christian and yet the evidence of *not* stepping up showed my lack faith.

I absolutely believe God works in all of our lives. However, I have been guilty of tunnel vision by only seeing God working in other people's lives and forgetting what He has done in mine. Watching others step out in faith and have their prayers answered while I didn't see the same in my life left me feeling that really ugly word—jealous. I got discouraged and I positioned myself as a spectator. I did this for years with my job. I saw and admired others who were in a career that God called them to. Their joy and passion were enviable, but I had one big problem: I didn't know my calling. I wondered if I was absent on the day God handed out callings, and I sat back as a spectator not believing He was working in that part of my life.

Sister, have you ever felt that way? Like God forgot you and isn't working on answering your prayers? Maybe you've been praying for years for the right man to come into your life and you watch as your friends are getting married and having children. You want to be happy for them, but you question if God forgot you. Or what about the woman who has an autoimmune disease and she watches her physically healthy friends accomplish goals she can only dream of. Her limitations make her question God's work in her life. How can we handle these moments of discouragement and despair that keep us from seeing God doing good work in our lives?

Let's go back to the story of the man by the pool in the book of John. The Jewish leaders who watched Jesus heal the man by the pool were very upset that Jesus had healed him on the Sabbath. They didn't have the correct view of how, why, and when God works and they wanted Jesus to follow their religious rules. How often do we do the very same thing? We are looking for God's work and answer to prayers to fit into our box, and if it doesn't, we assume He isn't working. But the Bible goes on to say, "But Jesus replied, 'My Father never stops working, so why should I?'" (John 5:17).

The truth is that God is always active. He never slumbers nor is He bound by time or space or any human condition. The Bible tells us, "He never grows faint or weary. No one can measure the depths of his understanding" (Isaiah 40:28). God never gets tired of working on our behalf and His strength does not diminish, but even more amazing is that God is working in our lives regardless of whether we recognize it or not. His work may not fit into our box and it isn't dependent upon us, however, the lack of seeing Him working in our lives could be the spectator view from which we are standing.

If we are spectators, we will not experience God in the same way that our faith-walking sisters do. Think of being at an amusement park watching as the gutsy people jump on the roller coaster. You can see what they are doing and you can imagine what it feels like, but you will never know for yourself unless you get on the ride. The same is true of faith. You can stand by and watch others walk in faith and see God working but never experience Him for yourself. On the other hand, the people who see God working in their lives are those who took a faith risk. When we move from refusing to act to stepping in faith, we literally change the lens we see Him through. Like putting on a pair of magnifying glasses, everything gets much easier to see. Stepping up and acting in faith is the key to changing our view of God and seeing His work in our lives.

I am sure if I were sitting next to you discussing these excuses, you could add a few more. We all have them, and to move towards the transformed life we want, we've got to come clean. Admitting and confessing our excuses is the first step to deflating their power in our lives. Sure, it is difficult to

Stepping up and acting in faith is the key to changing our view of God and seeing His work in our lives.

face the truth. In fact, excuses may be a result of wanting the easier path. Stepping up requires guts, a boldness that surpasses our own strength. However, isn't our God the same God who told the man laying by the pool to get up and walk and then, by faith, healed him? Let's take all our excuses and lay them at the feet of Christ and in faith, step up.

Transformation might be a single step away if we'd only let go of the excuses that hold us back.

Facing the excuses that prevent us from stepping up to the plate of our lives is part of the transformation journey. When I finally stepped up and quit my job, I experienced victory over the excuses that were holding me back. Their power got weaker as my faith got stronger. Don't be fooled—it doesn't take a lot of faith, just faith the size of a mustard seed (Matthew 17:20). Sister, there is victory for you, too.

By now you might be wondering what happened that awful day my mother died. It was one of the most difficult moments to either step up or give up. Deciding to step up meant becoming an adult overnight, and an adult I became. Quickly, I began making phone calls. First, to the mortgage company who kindly agreed to hold off on foreclosing so long as we immediately put the house on the market. Then to the electric company—they too were understanding and kept the electricity on knowing that once the house sold, they would get paid. Then phone calls to the doctors and hospital. An attorney was needed to clear the title on the house, and of course a realtor to sell the house. Not to mention, my dear little sister, only thirteen years old, who lived with me and was now my responsibility. When I look back on that time period, there is no way I got through it on my own. Bearing the burden of the estate, my sister's well-being, and my grief, I believe God literally carried me.

I could have taken the passive road and given into overwhelming grief. No one would have blamed me or thought less of me. I was too young to be facing a situation like this and how would I have known how to deal with things like selling a house, paying bills, getting an attorney, and managing the entire process on my own? After my mother's death I had a choice to either let the challenges before me play out or step up and take action. Maybe today you are facing crossroads where you could either step up or give up, and I completely understand how difficult it can be, but I believe you can make the faith choice to trust God and step up.

Sister, I guarantee you that stepping up won't be easy, but I also guarantee you that if you don't, your life will not change. God calls us to a life of faith, and faith is shown in our actions and the ability to move forward and trust God despite our fears and anxieties. I once heard it said, "God is waiting for you to move. Faith is you moving and trusting God."[6] It's bold, it's brave, it's necessary, and it's *Chickening IN*! It's okay if you're afraid. I am often afraid, too, but we don't have to let fear control us. We can face our fear and we can step up to our lives because of the One we trust in. "Because the Sovereign LORD helps me, I will not be disgraced. Therefore, I have set my face like a stone, determined to do his will" (Isaiah 50:7).

So how are you doing on the *Chickening IN* journey so far? I am praying that you are learning and growing and being empowered by God. This far, we've dived into facing our fear and stepping up to the plate of our life, which are both risky and risk is scary. But we can reduce the fear of risk by being smart risk-takers. There is no sense in being irrational and emotionally charged risk-takers, but rather we can be strategic and calculated.

ACTION STEPS:

1. Ponder a situation in which you regret not stepping up. Why did you decide not to take action? What would you do differently if you could have a do-over?

2. Think about the list of excuses: the timing isn't right, it's too hard, it's not my fault, or God isn't really working in my life. What excuses have you struggled with that have prevented you from stepping up in faith and taking responsibility?

3. Consider John 5:1-9. How would this man's life have been different if he didn't get up, pick up his mat, and walk when Jesus told him to? What can you learn from this story?

willing to take strategic risks to move towards a better life. Being wise in all things and knowing when to step out in faith.

Chapter 4

PILLAR #3 - TAKING CALCULATED RISKS

RISK IS A NECESSARY PART of life. Without risk, greatness cannot be achieved. In fact, America would not exist if not for the men and women willing to risk their lives for independence. Throughout the Bible we see people willing to risk their reputation, their possessions, their homes, their relationships, and their lives for God and to spread the greatest news anyone could ever hear—the gospel of Christ. Risk is essential to the Christian life and is needed to walk in faith. We all risk every day whether we know it or not: getting into a car to drive to work, telling someone how you really feel, or trusting God that a bad day will get better. Without risk change wouldn't happen. So far on this *Chickening IN* journey we've learned to *Face Our Fear* and to *Step Up to the Plate of Our Lives,* but there are still six more steps in the process, and in this chapter we will transform the way we approach risk taking, and we will learn nine simple steps to creating a risk strategy.

Risk is woven into the fiber of our best possible life, yet we try to avoid it at all costs. Risk is exposure to possible negative outcomes, and because we cannot know the outcome, we refuse to take chances. We're afraid of loss, pain, injury, vulnerability, and danger. But just as we fear the worst if we don't take a risk, by not taking chances we still risk failure. We risk living unfulfilled lives, we gamble with never reaching our potential, and we chance living a life full of regrets. By avoiding the possible *negative* outcomes of risk we ensure we will not experience the possible *positive* outcomes.

There are two types of risk: reckless risk and calculated risk. Reckless risk is irrational and careless. It's a choice that does not heed to caution or wisdom. It's giving into a sudden urge or impulse without thinking through the consequences, and it is usually accompanied by regret. Many of us can probably think of a family or friend who lives a reckless lifestyle. They are easy to identify because of their irrational decisions and the wreckage this type of behavior leaves behind. Often family members are left to pick up the broken pieces, pay off financial debt, or give this person a place to live.

For most, reckless risk is not a lifestyle, but a moment in time when common sense and good judgement are thrown to the wind. It won't come as a big surprise that teenagers are known for taking these types of risks. It is partially due to the development of their brains that causes the inability to foresee the future consequences of such behavior. My teen years certainly included a few reckless risks like skipping school, talking to the boy who was up to no good, and driving in a car with kids going too fast. But reckless risks are not limited to teens—adults are guilty, too. It might be quitting a job before a new one is secured, agreeing to marry someone just because you're growing weary and want a family, or wanting something so bad that you compromise God's best. This is the type of risk we want to avoid. The Bible says, "Zeal without knowledge is not good; a person who moves too quickly may go the wrong way" (Proverbs 19:2).

Since risk is a necessary part of life but we know that we want to avoid taking reckless risks, how can we risk wisely? The solution is calculated risks. Calculated risks are the exact opposite of reckless risks. It's not careless or impulsive, but rather strategic, well planned, and thought through. It's a risk taken with the full awareness of the potential consequences, and instead of making a snap decision, a calculated risk is a process in which we take a deep breath and pauses before jumping. Strategy is at the center of calculated risks, and by making a game plan we can reduce the exposure to negative outcomes. I want to reiterate that we cannot eliminate all negative outcomes but minimize them because risk itself is taking a chance, and there are no guarantees when we take chances.

Strategy is a useful skill that works hand in hand with taking calculated risks. Often when I think of strategy, the military comes to mind. The men and women in combat face great danger and their lives are at risk. To minimize the risks, they execute strategy by studying their enemy, learning the terrain, considering failure points, and mastering combat techniques that increase their odds of a successful mission.

In my business sales career, I had to implement strategy, too. It was my job to create and execute a well-thought-out plan to increase the odds of winning a sale. Throughout my fifteen-year career I learned how to slow down and move with intention. Every step or action had an order and purpose and trying to close a deal too soon was risky. Strategy was critical to my success because the risk of failure could be costly both to my purse and my employment status. Using strategy is not reserved just for the military or a sales career, but it is a skill we can incorporate into our personal lives to help us risk wisely, too.

We also can find strategy in the Bible, and Queen Esther is a great example of being strategically minded and taking a calculated risk. When we first meet Queen Esther, she is not yet royalty, but through a series of God-orchestrated events, a simple Jewish girl becomes the Queen of Persia. Upon wise advice from her cousin Mordecai, Esther had withheld her true identity from the King. Now as Queen she was well-positioned to do great things—but great things are not necessarily easy and sometimes require an enormous amount of courage.

Queen Esther had no idea that, while in the palace, she would face the biggest challenge of her life. It started when the king promoted Haman to second in charge next to himself. Haman was an arrogant and prideful man who demanded respect. He required that all the king's officials bow down and honor him. Mordecai was Jewish and refused to do so, and in anger Haman went to the king and persuaded the king to issue a decree to annihilate the Jews. Let's pause for a second—it's worthy to note that Mordecai showed a great deal of courage by refusing to bow to Haman. Jews were not to worship anyone except the God of the Bible, and Mordecai was willing to risk it all to stand for his beliefs. Have you ever been in a situation where what was being asked of you went against your Christian beliefs? These can be costly situations that result in the loss of your reputation, relationships, or even a job or a position. Mordecai found the strength to risk because he knew who he was. You, too, can find courage during times like this by remembering your identity in Christ. The Bible says, "For I can do everything through Christ, who gives me strength" (Philippians 4:13).

Mordecai was devastated and went into mourning. Queen Esther soon learned about Mordecai's grief and the decree issued by her husband to kill all the Jews. She knew her life and the lives of all her people were in grave danger. She had a choice to make: remain quiet, save her life, and hope for the best, or go before the king, reveal her identity, and plead her case. It was a big risk to go before the king when he had not requested her presence, one that could result in her death. Her first reaction was self-preservation and isn't that just like all of us. Rather than stand up and intervene, we sit in the shadows hoping we can escape exposure and that God will work it out. Fear is always at the core of self-preservation. I had a situation happen in my workplace with a leader who didn't lead with integrity. Instead this person led with intimidation, loyalty only to self, and the prideful assumption that she was always right. Many of my coworkers, including myself were victims of her yelling fits. No one was willing to do anything because we were all afraid of losing our jobs. The unwillingness to risk allowed this behavior to continue and it fostered an unhealthy environment, and an unhealthy me. I was frustrated all the time and I did everything I could to avoid this person—even to the point of not wanting to go to work at all. Thankfully, this leader was demoted and eventually left the company, but not before many of my co-workers moved on to new jobs.

During times of fear, self-preservation, and retreat, we often need someone to speak encouragement into our lives—a friend, mentor, or coach—someone to wake us up or shake us up. That's exactly what Mordecai did for Queen Esther when he spoke these wise and powerful words, "What's more, who can say but that you have been elevated to the palace for just such a time as this" (Esther 4:14)? This is the most well-known verse in the book of Esther and for good reason. Esther was in a position of influence unlike anyone else. Her identity as a Jew had been concealed. She was beautiful and found favor with the king. She had learned the customs of the palace and understood how to behave in her new culture. What appeared to be many coincidences was actually God's providence for the Jewish people—Esther was positioned for this moment.

Have you ever experienced being positioned well and you knew it was your time to execute? It was as if God prepared you all along through your past, your resources, and your relationships lining up, and what seemed disconnected was coming together for a single purpose. That is exactly what Mordecai was saying to Esther.

Using my life as an example, I told the story earlier of a nonprofit job that I really wanted to take but ultimately fear got the best of me. If I were sitting in front of you right now, I would lean in and look you in your eyes just so you could see my sincerity when I say this:

> My heart breaks. The opportunity to make a big impact on women's lives was within one word. My career skills and experience were a match, my walk with Christ was maturing to a point that I cared more about people and purpose than six figures, the nonprofit agency was excited to have someone with my talents, the relationship with the leaders was evidence of God's hand moving, and the job offer was confirmation. I try not to read too much

into signs and wonders, but in this case there were too many to deny. Everywhere I went the name of the organization was either being promoted or spoken about, and it was personal, too. One night, as I ate dinner at a restaurant, I came out and found a pamphlet for the nonprofit on my car windshield. It was as if God was talking directly to me, giving me the courage I needed, and I could not deny this opportunity was from Him. *For such a time as this* . . . it rings in my ears because I chose self-preservation and fear over taking a faith risk. I pray that this chapter on calculated risks will propel you to say *yes* when a "for such a time as this" moment comes into your life.

Esther's story was much different than mine, and upon hearing Mordecai's advice she was instantly transformed by the knowledge that God had placed her in the palace for this very reason: to save her people. Her mindset shifted from self to others, and Esther, once a meek, young girl, was now a courageous, decisive leader. She recognized her purpose and quickly started planning to take a calculated risk.

I love what happens next. Esther isn't careless or rushed to go before the king. That is a hard concept for our fast-paced culture. We don't like waiting five minutes for our coffee let alone waiting and preparing for the right job, right ministry, right spouse, or right timing for the good things God has for us. It says in Proverbs that "a prudent person foresees danger and takes precautions. The simpleton goes blindly on and suffers the consequences" (Proverbs 27:12). Esther knew going before the king was a life or death risk and she had to proceed carefully. Her plan was strategic, specific, and it took longer than just one day. She knew she would need an enormous amount of courage and faith to execute her calculated risk.

The first step was gathering all the Jews and asking them to fast with her for three days. Fasting was an act that took their minds off their fear and shifted their focus to God. This is important for us to hear—Esther gathered others and she paused. When faced with fearful, risky, faith walking decisions, how often do you rally other Christians to fast or pray with you? Do you take time to pause and focus on God and His Word? Taking risks is like going into a war zone of fearful what-ifs, and the enemy is ready to launch you into confusion. By taking a step back and seeking God with others, He can and will prepare you to face risks head on with wisdom, discernment, and Spirit-filled strength.

The strategy continues as Esther prepares herself to catch the attention of the king. She puts on her royal robes—I imagine her trying everything possible to look her best and paying attention to the smallest of details. Strategy lends itself to picky specifics whereas rushing overlooks the small, assuming it's trivial. Queen Esther knew every detail counted towards success. She entered the palace well prepared. Are you a well-prepared risk taker, or do you skimp on the details? In my business sales career, the bigger the sales proposal the more articulate we had to be about why, how, and what, because strategy is the art of honing in on the most important elements to increase the likelihood of success. The bigger the risk the more attention that needs to go towards the details.

Queen Esther's efforts paid off because the king noticed her and invited her with his scepter. She requested his attendance at a banquet and the king accepted. But again, Esther didn't rush into pleading with the king at the banquet. She was poised and requested a second banquet. All the while God was working behind the scenes and God's favor was upon her. Think about this: Esther had to be shaking with fear for her life, and yet she remained calm and confident. She was taking a calculated risk and doing it afraid. Take notice that with proper planning and preparation we can feel afraid on the inside while presenting confidence on the outside. We can do that because God did not give us a spirit of fear, but rather one of power and self-control (2 Timothy 1:7).

The time came for Esther to risk it all. All her preparation and strategy brought her to the moment of truth when the king said, "Tell me what you want, Queen Esther. What is your request" (Esther 7:2)? It was time for

> That is Chickening IN! Approaching risks with wisdom and understanding, and then, when the time is right being able to step in faith, take the risk, and trust God with the outcome.

Esther to plead for the lives of the Jews as well as her own. When your "risk it all moment" comes, how do you handle it? Do you go for it or do you retreat? Planning and strategy prepared her, but she still had to jump without knowing what the outcome would be. That is *Chickening IN*! Approaching risks with wisdom and understanding, and then, when the time is right being able to step in faith, take the risk, and trust God with the outcome. In our lifetime, we may or may not face a life-threatening risk but we all face everyday risks like failure, loss, embarrassment, or exposure, and like Esther, we can implement a plan, patiently wait for right timing, and invite others to help us. By doing so, we transform the way in which we risk and posture ourselves in a much more favorable position to succeed. That is what calculated risk is all about.

If it were that easy to create a plan and take calculated risks, why don't we follow our dreams, pursue our God-given purpose, walk in faith, and take chances more often and with ease? I am going to take a risky guess and say that most us are not familiar with strategic planning. If it weren't for my job in strategic sales, I would feel uncomfortable with the idea of strategy, too. But this is a skill everyone can learn and a skill that will change the way you think. I am confident of that. Risk strategy is simple with these nine steps. I've used them many times, and most recently with my risk to quit my career and reinvent myself as a writer. You can use them, too.

1. IDENTIFY THE RISK

The first step in strategic planning is to identify the risk you need to take. For Queen Esther, it was approaching the king uninvited and pleading with him to not kill the Jews. In my previous career, the risk was creating a proposal and pitching it to the customer with the hope of winning a large deal. If I failed to win, it could ultimately result in the loss of my job. Now in my writing career, the risk was quitting my sales career to become a successful published author and to homeschool my daughter. For you, it might be starting a new business, changing jobs, or something completely different like going back to school, homeschooling your children, speaking at a women's group, or maybe even something difficult like leaving an abusive relationship. Whatever it is, the more specific you can be the better. Write down your risk and be specific. What risk do you want to take but are too afraid to?

2. GAIN WISDOM AND UNDERSTANDING

Strategic planning includes gaining knowledge and understanding about the risk. Before a big risk is taken it is vitally important that research about the topic is done first. It says in Proverbs that "getting wisdom is the wisest thing you can do! And whatever else you do, develop good judgement" and "if you instruct the wise, they will be all the wiser" (Proverbs 4:7; 21:11). Spend time researching and learning about the topic. Queen Esther already had the expertise of knowing the king's preferences and mannerisms. She also knew the laws and the acceptable ways to approach the king. If she didn't know this information, she could have made a big mistake and the result could have been deadly. The same was true in my business sales career. I had to research my customer to know their business and their culture to give myself credibility and increase my potential of winning a sale. Find out what you don't know. Become an expert in the subject matter and grow in wisdom and knowledge—then you will have good judgement.

3. GATHER COMMUNITY AROUND YOU

The Bible says, "Plans succeed through good counsel; don't go to war without wise advice" (Proverbs 20:18). Queen Esther quickly gathered others. Not just anyone but her people, the Jews. When making strategic plans we need the advice of others who are trusted, who are experts in the area of the change we want to make, or whose motive is solely to help. We need people who love and trust God. Wisdom and encouragement can be found in community. Praying and fasting together is a powerful act of faith. Also, sharing best practices will boost your courage and your ability to take risks.

4. IDENTIFY ROADBLOCKS

Considering potential roadblocks is necessary to good planning. The Bible encourages us and says "the wise are cautious and avoid danger" (Proverbs 14:16). We are wise if we take time to identify anything that might prevent us from taking the risk. It could be tangible items like money, physical resources, or people. But also take into account internal roadblocks like feelings of fear, worry, or a lack of self-confidence. For Queen Esther, she understood that timing was a potential roadblock, and if she moved too quickly it could be detrimental. In business sales when presenting a proposal, I had to consider possible customer objections that could prevent the customer from saying *yes*. You most likely have experienced this when talking to a person trying to sell you a product—with every reason you have for not purchasing the product, the salesperson has a reason why you need the product or a rebuttal, and a really good one. By creating our own personal rebuttals to every roadblock and proactively planning to deflect them, we can overcome the roadblocks that might prevent us from taking the needed or desired risk.

5. KNOW YOUR ENEMY

Knowing your enemy is as important as understanding roadblocks. Haman was certainly the enemy to the Jews, and Queen Esther had to strategically consider what impact he might have upon her risk to see the king. She knew Haman liked to be honored so she thoughtfully invited him to the second banquet. We need to honestly assess our enemy. It is true our enemy will try every tactic to keep us from taking leaps of faith. He doesn't want the name of Jesus to be exalted, and Satan is pleased when we are bound up with fear, worry, and doubt. His entry point in our lives is through our weaknesses and he will try to influence our thoughts in these areas. The Bible says, "He prowls around like a roaring lion, looking for someone to devour" (1 Peter 5:8). We need to expect the enemy to attack us just like the helpless animal, but to also remember that we can resist the devil when joined with Christ and he will flee when we draw close to God with a humble heart (James 4:7-8). Satan's influence is temporary and short-lived, and knowing the victory is already won in Christ can give us strength.

6. KNOW YOUR WEAKNESS

Everyone has weaknesses. Denying them can sabotage strategy but acknowledging weaknesses will pave the way to overcome them. Queen Esther's weakness was her position in relation to the king. She did not have ultimate power or authority, and by understanding her status, she approached the situation with careful humility. For me, the company I worked for had its product weaknesses and addressing them meant the difference between winning or losing the sale. I struggled for years to confess that I wanted to be a writer—my lack of self-confidence was one of my weaknesses. But God is greater than any weakness; the Bible says, "My grace is all you need. My power works best in weakness" (2 Corinthians 12:9). Our weakness in the hands of God can become the tool He uses to do great things through us. But we first must admit our weaknesses and confess them to God. With a sober mind we need to consider how these weaknesses affect our ability to take risk and with prayer, lay them at the feet of Christ.

7. FOCUS ON THE POSITIVE

While calculated risks involve considering the possible negative outcomes, it's more important to focus on the possible positive outcomes. The knowledge that she could save the lives of the Jewish people gave Queen

Esther unwavering courage to step up. For you personally, if your mind lingers on the potential for disaster you will never muster up the courage to take risks; however, by placing your thoughts on what's good and possible, hope will emerge, and you will become a successful risk taker. The Bible encourages us to take bad thoughts captive and view ourselves in the light of Christ because we have very powerful minds. So often what we think leads to how we feel, and how we feel leads to action. By focusing on the positive outcomes, we can impact our feelings and actions and become faith walkers and smart risk takers.

8. TAKE SMALL DOABLE STEPS

Every plan is a series of small steps. No one goes from a fast-food cashier to a restaurant owner overnight. Even the most seasoned leader or well-trained athlete started at the bottom and worked to their position one step at a time. A good strategy will include many small steps. Queen Esther understood this principle as well—she didn't rush into pleading with the king, but articulated small steps to get her there. Strategic sales planning is no different. When I won a very large sale it wasn't because of one action; it was a culmination of many smaller actions that added up to the bigger outcome. Why would we approach taking personal risks any other way? By breaking it down into doable steps it deflates some of the fear. In Proverbs 3:21-23, we are instructed not to lose sight of good planning. It provides safety, it will keep your feet from stumbling, and it will provide relief from fear and anxiety that keeps us up at night. Small steps might look like this: your heart is leading you to speak at a large women's conference, but you're terrified of getting up in front of an audience. Start small by preparing a speech for an audience of one—yourself. Then move on to two people, and gradually take steps toward a larger audience. Enroll in a speech class or join a local Toastmasters, an international nonprofit that promotes communication and public speaking. Watch other speakers and learn how they overcame the fear of speaking in front of large crowds. Attend a speaker's conference and read books about the subject. By breaking it down into small, practical steps, your roadblock becomes unobstructed and achievable, thus reducing the fear and anxiety of the risk.

9. TAKE THE LEAP OF FAITH!

The final step to risk strategy is *Chickening IN* and just doing it. Everything you have planned and prepared for is done. Gaining wisdom, gathering community, confessing your weakness, focusing on the positive outcomes, and studying possible roadblocks have led to this moment—the ultimate moment of surrendering to the unknown and taking the risk. With risk strategy under your feet, it's time to take a leap of faith, trust God, and take your calculated risk. Remember you are never alone. The Bible says, "Don't be afraid, for I am with you. Don't be discouraged, for I am your God. I will strengthen you and help you. I will hold you up with my victorious right hand" (Isaiah 41:10). God is with us—giving us the strength to risk and walk in faith and regardless of the outcome, our faith in Christ will produce a victory because we have trusted Him.

It's worthy to note that, at times, you may be presented with a risky decision in which there is no time to strategize. Personally, I prefer not to make rushed decisions that involve risk, but situations like this do happen. What should we do? Start with Jesus—He is only a whisper away. Call out to Him under your breath and ask Him for wisdom. If possible, try to get five or ten minutes alone to pray and make a quick pros/cons list. Maybe text or call your spouse or trusted friend for a quick review. I call this a mini-strategy session, and it will help. However, as much as possible, avoid making *quick* risky decisions. Maybe ask for more time, but if that isn't possible and you don't have an answer, then you will have to go

> God is with us—giving us the strength to risk and walk in faith and regardless of the outcome, our faith in Christ will produce a victory because we have trusted Him.

with your gut instinct. I tend to err on the side of caution unless there is very compelling evidence that this risk decision is right for me.

We are now armed with a risk strategy plan that will help us be smart risk takers, but there is still one more question we must address. It is critically important to have the courage to take the last step in the risk strategy plan—a leap of faith. But *where does your security lie?* Is it misplaced or God-placed? If security in earthly things is elevated above God, then taking leaps of faith and risking will be very difficult, even with a risk strategy.

Unfortunately, our culture is growing more and more safety obsessed. We try to avoid or prevent bad things from happening by adding new laws, family rules, or letting our fears guide us. We're afraid of catching a virus, being the victim of a crime, losing our job, having no food, or being left out in the cold. And because we are so safety-minded, we go to great lengths to feel secure. We take prevention medicine, we don't go out after dark, and we purchase bulk food to overfill our kitchen cabinets, all to help relieve the tension of feeling that life is on a slippery slope and that if we can prevent bad things we can feel more at ease.

It's important to realize that our plight to prevent bad things from happening will never be satisfied. The Bible tells us that "in this world you will have trouble" (John 16:33, NIV). The world is not suitable to handle our security needs, and since life is ever changing, we should avoid putting our security in a job, in a reputation, in a position or in money. Even with her royal position in the palace, Queen Esther wasn't secure. I am not saying to abandon all wisdom and good sense—that would be going against God, too. But consider that maybe our security is misplaced, and because it is misplaced it is stealing our ability to walk in faith, trust God, and take needed risks.

Yes, it is true that the Bible tells us we will have trouble, but I didn't share the entire verse. There is more—the part where God encourages us to have courage and peace, and while we will have struggles the ultimate victory has been won. Victory over death! Jesus continues and says, "I have told you these things, so that in me you may have peace. In this world you will have trouble. But take heart! I have overcome the world" (John 16:33, NIV).

The bigger question for us today is where is our security placed? By taking the risk to see the king, Queen Esther confirmed her security was in God alone. She understood God's providence. For us, do we really believe God cares for us, protects us, and His plan will prevail in our lives? Do we believe in luck and coincidences or do we believe that God's guiding hand is orchestrating and lining up circumstances for our good? Security in anything but God will eventually fail us. He is the firm foundation by which we can take risks and walk in faith. It's comforting and it gives us courage to know that regardless of the success or failure of the risk that God works all things out for the good of those who love Him (Romans 8:28).

When we are too earthly minded, it seems very risky to put our security in God alone. However, God's ways are opposite of the world's ways and security in anything other than the One who can give us eternal life will fail us. This shift in our thinking combined with the nine steps of risk strategy planning will give us the means to take calculated risks. I know, I hear you— risk is moving into the land of the unknown and the unknown is very scary. I warned you in the first chapter that *Chickening IN* isn't for the faint of heart. This is hard stuff—really trusting God and walking in faith is so much more than lip service, it is action and it involves risk.

ACTION STEPS:

1. What kind of risk taker are you? Are you reckless, calculated, or do you not take risks at all?

2. What is one risk if you could not fail that you would want to take? Can you put together a risk strategy plan for that?

3. Is your security misplaced or God-placed?

willingness to "go" or "do" the unfamiliar. Ability to tolerate the unknown knowing God is with you, leading you. Dare to go beyond your comfort zone.

Chapter 5

PILLAR #4 - TRAVELING DOWN UNKNOWN ROADS

TRAVELING IS A TRILLION-DOLLAR GLOBAL industry. People travel for work and for pleasure both locally and to foreign countries. Most likely you have traveled, too. Most of us look forward to traveling because it is exciting and can give us a much-needed break. For those who travel a lot, you understand that it is a skill and the more you practice, the better you are at navigating the ins and outs of traveling. For some, traveling brings up feelings of fear such as the fear of flying or going to a foreign country. Going to new places can make us vulnerable because we are in unfamiliar surroundings, and that alone can cause us to decide to stay home. Living a life of courage and faith is much like traveling. When we decide to follow God, we will be faced with traveling down new roads and taking leaps of faith never before imagined. It might be a personal road of recovery or following a calling God has on your life. To be prepared, we need to learn to travel well, travel often, and have the courage to plunge into the unknown.

So far on our *Chickening IN* journey we've learned to face our fears, step up to the plate of our lives, and to take calculated risks. You may notice this is a stepping-stone process and each pillar of *Chickening IN* is intertwined with the others. This next step is no different. Pillar three, taking calculated risks, prepared us for pillar four, walking roads we've never been on before. I call it **Traveling Unknown Roads.** To truly walk in faith and live a courageous life we've got to be willing to embrace the unknown. All it takes is a first step of faith, but letting go of the familiar and surrendering to the unknown is harder than it sounds. Being skilled travelers will help us, and to do that we must unpack the major roadblock that prevents us from embarking into uncharted territory and understand where the fear is coming from and how to manage it.

The greatest enemy to the unknown is the familiar. To gain more insight of why we are so drawn to the familiar, let's define what *known* means. It's a state of familiarity or established knowledge. It's being clear or certain about a person, experience, or outcome. It's more than knowledge of, it's personal experience that makes it known. For example, if you have heard cupcakes are sweet that is just knowledge, but if you have tasted them, then the sweetness of cupcakes is known to you. Once something is known it can become familiar, comfortable, expected, and safe.

Have you ever noticed that most Target stores are laid out exactly the same? When you walk in the front door, the dollar bins are conveniently right in front, the women's department is on the left, women's accessories on the other side of the aisle from the dollar bins, and the girl's clothing is across from the registers. This is one of many reasons why I love Target. It is predictable, reliable, and known to me. When I enter, I know exactly what direction to walk to get what I need. No hassles. No going up and down aisles trying to find the dental floss or the paper towels. However, on rare occasions, I have gone into a Target store that has a different layout, and honestly I don't like it. Not knowing which direction to go can be frustrating, awkward, and at times intimidating. Isn't it so true? There's something comforting about the predictable, not just at Target but in life as well.

The known allows us to go on auto pilot. There is safety in the reliability of the known even when the known is boring, unhealthy, or not God's will for our life. Sure, there are situations where the known is exactly what we need. Kids thrive in a family environment with regular routines. But

> It's on the unfamiliar, unknown road that we are stripped of our dependence on self and the idols we have created in our hearts, and we are forced to fully rely on God.

there are times when the known causes a major roadblock to our faith and our trust in God. We refuse to heed to the prompting from God to travel an unknown road and we miss out on His best. Sister, I hear you. The familiar is safe, but the problem is that God rarely calls His people to travel the familiar and routine roads. **It's on the unfamiliar, unknown road that we are stripped of our dependence on self and the idols we have created in our hearts, and we are forced to fully rely on God.**

God has called me to walk on unknown paths many times. In fact, I can depend on God to point me toward them. I imagine Him lovingly speaking these words under His breath as I once again resist His guidance towards taking risks: *Trust me. My motive is pure and good. I want what's best for you. Follow me.* Getting out of my safety zone and stepping onto unknown pathways has taken a lot of courage—more than I could muster up myself. Learning to trust God and let go has challenged my sense of security, causing me to reconsider who or what I believe most, and it has revealed my misplaced trust in the familiar things of this world.

Six weeks into the first grade God made it clear that I needed to withdraw my youngest daughter, Hope, from private Christian school and homeschool her. I never envisioned myself homeschooling, and just like writing, every fear and doubt possible regarding my inadequacies came flooding in—*I am not educated enough, I will ruin her life, I am not the teacher type . . . .really God?* Yet that is exactly the unknown route He was directing my feet to travel.

I was a full-time working mom and Hope started preschool when she was three years old. Separation anxiety seemed like a normal reaction for a first-time preschooler, but as time went on it got louder, stronger, and more difficult to manage. By the time she entered first grade, her separation anxiety peaked, and every day as she entered the classroom she did what I call the "Spiderman." Basically she sprawled out with hands and feet gripping the doorway as if her life depended upon it. Maybe she was afraid of her strict, not so warm-and-fuzzy teacher, maybe it was the tummy ache every morning on the car ride to school, or that she got head lice, and I must not forget the hives that required a trip to the ER. Or maybe my work and travel schedule was too overwhelming for a little girl who wanted her mom. The exact reason didn't matter because this was God's way of getting my attention. He was using these extreme circumstances to call me away from the comfort of the known to begin a new chapter of life. After much prayer, seeking wisdom from other homeschool moms, talking to her doctor, and the school, my husband, David, and I made the boldest parenting move we've ever made. I withdrew Hope from school and we became a homeschool family.

As I left the school campus that day, I had no idea what was coming next. I was traveling an unknown road with the hope of a better life for my daughter and a better future for my family. It was surreal, almost as if I were watching myself like a bystander and wondering who this crazy lady was. Homeschooling was God's plan for my daughter's life. It was God's way to cause our family to slow down and consider what was really important. I was absolutely terrified. In fact, four years later I am still scared that I am not doing a good enough job. But then I remind myself it is God who called me to the unknown path of homeschooling, and He is guiding me each step of the way. This road might be unknown to me but not to God. Trust—that is what God is calling me to, a deeper trust in Him.

The Scriptures are full of examples of God calling everyday people to walk unknown roads, to have faith and trust in God's plan without seeing how it will turn out. Author John Ortberg says, "Very rarely does God come to someone and say, 'Stay.' Almost never does God interrupt someone and ask them to remain in comfort, safety, and familiarity. He opens a door and calls them to come through it."[7] God called Abraham and Sarah to leave the familiar and comfortable place in which they lived. Having no idea exactly what that meant, they began traveling on an unknown road. Hebrews tells us that "it was by faith that Abraham obeyed when God called him to leave home and go to another land that God would give him as his inheritance. He went without knowing where he was going" (Hebrews 11:8). John Ortberg says, "You never know where you are going if you are going by faith."[8]

Taking risks, living with courage, and following God will most likely lead to unfamiliar roads. There are many kinds of unknown roads. Think of them not just as physical places, but mental, emotional, and spiritual places you've never been. Most often they will steer us to climb steep mountains, cross desert plains, sail uncharted oceans, or soar to new heights. If we are willing to travel these unknown roads we will be challenged by our fears and doubts and we may be tempted to turn back. However, if we refuse to give in to the fear bully, we might discover something new and amazing about ourselves, God, and life.

Are you reluctant to take risks and travel to unknown places? It could be moving to a new city or a mid-life career change. It could be pursuing healing in a broken relationship or forgiving a grievance you've held onto for years. Maybe God is making it clear that big, bold changes need to happen at home, ones that are not culturally popular. Maybe it's a new road of learning to walk without a loved one who passed, or you yourself are facing a life-threatening diagnosis. Whatever it is, the Bible is full of encouragement to strengthen our trust and faith in God, and to give us the courage to *Chicken IN* and travel these unknown roads.

courage is contagious.

Courage is contagious. I know this to be true because it's happened many times and deciding to homeschool was one of those instances. Hearing stories from others who have faced the unknowns of home education reduced my fears and increased my courage to act. Their ability to walk down this road inspired and infected me with courage. Catching the courage bug was exactly what I needed to move from fear to faith and to step into the new life of homeschooling.

The same holds true for the unknown road I am on right now. I admire people who follow their dreams and pursue God's plans and purposes for their life. My husband, David, is one of those people. He knew early on in his life that his calling was to serve and protect as a law enforcement officer. Watching him over the years go from a dream, to the academy, and on to his career has inspired me. His actions gave me courage to follow my dreams.

The Bible has been the single most powerful source of courage and strength in my life. There are many stories of people who faced unknown roads, and by exploring their struggles and triumphs, their courage and faith can rub off on us and give us the inspiration we need to take risks and live in faith. **By digging into the Word, we position ourselves to catch the courage and faith of people like Moses, Joseph, and Daniel.** I believe that as you continue to read you will identify personally with their stories. My hope is that the next time we are at the crossroads of the familiar and the unknown that these examples will steer us away from fearfulness and towards trust in God.

UNSEEN AND INVISIBLE ROADS: MOSES

The Bible tells the story of Moses and the Israelites traveling the unknown road from slavery in Egypt to freedom in the Promised Land. Moses and the Israelites were well on their way when Pharaoh changed his mind and wanted them to return to Egypt. Pharaoh gathered his soldiers and charged after the Israelites. When the Israelites saw the Egyptian armies in the distance, they became afraid and angry because they saw no pathway to escape. They were trapped between the Red Sea and the Egyptian army and they began to reason that being a slave and alive was better than dying in the wilderness. Fear overcame their faith because they could not see what God was doing. Their minds were focused on the facts of their surroundings and they left God out of the equation.

Then Moses said, "Don't be afraid. Just stand still and watch the LORD rescue you today" (Exodus 14:13). **What the Israelites couldn't see was a pathway, an unknown road that God was making just for them. It was invisible to the human eye, but it was still there.** Then, "the LORD opened up a path through the water with a strong east wind" and it blew all night leaving a dry path for the Israelites (Exodus 14:21). God literally parted the Red Sea. Asaph, an author of some of the Psalms, writes, "your road led through the sea, your pathway through the mighty waters—a pathway no one knew was there" (Psalm 77:19)!

I wonder what the Israelites were thinking as they witnessed an invisible pathway become visible? God performed a miracle, but now it was up to them—they had to act. The Israelites had to be willing to travel this unknown road. It didn't look like any road they had walked before. This road had walls of water on each side. What were they thinking and feeling? Were they afraid the water would come crashing down on them? Did they fear the strong winds or that the land below them would give way? Did they question their physical strength and ability to get to the other side? Maybe they wanted to return to the familiar, to slavery in Egypt?

Returning to slavery was tempting. In fact, the Israelites lashed out at Moses and reasoned that they were better off alive and slaves in Egypt than free and wandering (Exodus 14:11-12). Think with me for a minute. Imagine if the Israelites would have surrendered to Pharaoh and returned back to Egypt. They were steps away from God's deliverance. Imagine missing out on walking through the Red Sea. Talk about traveling an unknown road— it doesn't get anymore unknown than stepping your foot onto the dry sea

> we don't have to see the end of the road, we just have to believe in the One who can.

floor with walls of ocean water on each side of you, then witnessing the ocean waters merging back together sweeping over the Egyptian army and killing them all.

So many times in my life I have hit barriers that have prevented me from trusting God. The road I was traveling was foreign and I could not fathom how God was going to make a pathway for my feet. Like the Israelites, looking back on the known and imagining that it was better than the unknown has filtrated my thoughts. Do you do this, too? When hope of a better future appears impossible and the situation looks grim, do you glorify the past as an excuse to return to the familiar and the comfortable? Though it is tempting to do so, this is not the time to give up. It's time to *Chicken IN* and embrace the unknown.

God is the God of invisible pathways—roads we cannot see with our eyes or imagine in our minds. In Isaiah it says, "'My thoughts are nothing like your thoughts,' says the Lord. 'And my ways are far beyond anything you could imagine'" (Isaiah 55:8). Faith is believing God has a way when it appears to be impossible. My dear sister, I know how difficult it is to take your eyes off of the facts, and I don't say this carelessly, but rather as a call to join me on this journey to trust God with our steps of faith into the unknown. **We don't have to see the end of the road, we just have to believe in the One who can.**

I DIDN'T CHOOSE THIS ROAD: JOSEPH

It was over twenty years ago that I first read about Joseph in Genesis, and all these years later I am still receiving encouragement and strength from this story to walk the unknown paths of life. Joseph is a prime example of being forced to go down an unknown and unexpected road that took him away from everything he was familiar with. In fact, he traveled multiple unknown roads including rejection, enslavement, and imprisonment. Though his journey began involuntarily, God used these unknown roads in mighty ways, and ultimately He positioned Joseph to save the lives of his family and to create the Israelite nation.

As a boy, Joseph's brothers were jealous of him and they devised a plan to get rid of him by throwing him into a deep pit. That pit was not chosen by Joseph, it was picked for him and it led Joseph to being sold into slavery. Do you think fear overcame Joseph? I wonder how hurt and confused he was by this sudden change of course. Have you ever felt that way? Without notice, life takes an unfair turn and there you find yourself living a life you didn't plan.

But God was with Joseph and His favor was upon him. Joseph worked hard, he didn't make excuses, and he made the best of his unknown road. Most of us would sink in self-pity and depression, but Joseph walked this road well. As a result, Joseph was promoted from slave to head of Potiphar's entire household. This is the kind of traveler I want to be.

Again with God's favor, Joseph was doing everything possible to honor Potiphar, but unfortunately another involuntary, unknown road was coming: prison. Potiphar's wife falsely accused Joseph of rape. I often wonder how Joseph managed his emotions through all of this. It can be devastating when you are making progress and then someone with ill intentions thwarts your plans. It's like getting kicked in the gut. But still God was with Joseph. The Bible says, "the LORD was with him and caused everything he did to succeed" (Genesis 39:23).

During Joseph's time behind bars, God gave him the ability to interpret dreams. His ability led him on another unknown road, but this road was God's plan all along. Pharaoh appointed Joseph second-in-command to himself. Joseph's life was a mosaic of many unknown roads, pathways he had no choice in making. But God was up to something. He was weaving together a plan. The unjust choices of others over Joseph's life did not overrule God's sovereignty.

Then, the "for such a time as this" moment that we learned about in the fourth chapter was coming full circle for Joseph just like it did for Esther. Joseph's brothers, who had sold him into slavery, unknowingly bowed before him. They didn't recognize him, but Joseph knew they were his brothers, the ones who threw him into a pit all those years ago. Can you imagine the intense emotions that Joseph might have felt? But what's most impressive about Joseph is his response. There's no blame or retaliation, no yelling or angry outburst. Instead, when Joseph revealed his identity to his family he said, "Don't be angry with yourselves for selling me into this place. It was God who sent me here ahead of you to preserve your lives" (Genesis 45:5). Joseph understood how God worked all his unknown roads together for Joseph's good.

Joseph's story is rich with encouragement. Joseph's life seemed to be that of a puppet being directed by the cruel intentions of others. He quickly went from freedom to enslavement and then to prison. But, the Bible says, "The LORD was with Joseph, so he succeeded in everything he did as he served in the home of his Egyptian master" (Genesis 39:2). Though Joseph was forced to walk a road he didn't choose, it did not mean that God had abandoned him or that he was to endure the hardships of this new life on his own. John Ortberg says in his book *All The Places to Go . . . How Will You Know?*, "Spiritual maturity is being able to face troubles without being troubled."[9] Joseph had every right to be angry, bitter, and depressed, but instead he chose to serve and to serve *well*. He chose to walk the road and own it. He brought his best into every situation regardless of how he got there.

I can identify with Joseph because as a young girl I felt that my life was on a confusing and unjust roadway. My mother's many marriages forced our family down unknown paths that led to abuse, neglect, and hardship. Then, cancer took her life—and all of this before I was eighteen years old. Much like Joseph, I had no control. I was forced to walk these roads.

Obviously, I was a child and children don't have the ability to control the roads their parents travel down, but after my mother's death I did have a choice to make. A choice to forgive, to own the situation, and to make the best of it. Or I could choose to remain a victim and let it destroy my future and my outlook on life.

How about you? Have you felt the harsh reality of being forced onto a pathway of life you didn't choose? We can find ourselves on these unchosen roads when a spouse has an affair, a loved one dies, or the actions of another person causes an unexpected change of direction. It's easy to refuse to own the road to recovery or to reinvent our life and create a new normal. It's easy to assume God isn't traveling these roads with us or that He has abandoned us, but Scripture doesn't support that. God was with Joseph and God is with you, too.

We must not skip over those words of Joseph to his family in Genesis 45:5: "Don't be angry with yourselves for selling me into this place. It was God who sent me here ahead of you to preserve your lives." Though tragedy forced Joseph down a hard, long road, God had a greater purpose in mind. Joseph recognized God's providence and he found peace. God can take anything that happens to us and turn it around for good if we will let Him.

Believe me, it has been a difficult, painful, and emotional unknown road for me. I didn't want to forgive my mother because I was deeply affected by the actions of her and her husbands. The consequences carried themselves into my adult life, my marriage, and my view of myself. I dealt with anxiety, depression, and a gaping hole in my heart. Undoing all the lies and learning to trust God has been an ongoing process. But years later, I am able to see how God is using my history to glorify His power in my life. Please remember, I didn't get there overnight. But I can say without a doubt that God has been with me, showering me with His love, and redeeming my brokenness.

Can you look back and recognize God turning an unexpected, unknown road around for good? Many times God will take our pain and use it to help others facing a similar injustice. I think of amazing women who have suffered physical abuse and are now free of it and are mentoring women through their own healing journey. Or moms who have walked the unknown road of a disabled or a terminally ill child, and their experience allows them to emphatically comfort other moms with a listening ear, tissues, and a shoulder to lean on. It's not easy to see how God will use unjust, unknown roads for a bigger purpose, but when the time is right and our heart is ready I believe He will reveal it. If God can use Joseph's unchosen roads, He can use yours, too.

OBEDIENCE TO GOD AND RIGHT ROADS: DANIEL

I wonder what the road of obedience looked and felt like for Daniel. Daniel had always prayed to God three times a day. But now with the new law from King Darius the Mede, he was restricted from his prayer life for thirty days. The Bible says, "But when Daniel learned that the law had been signed, he went home and knelt down as usual in his upstairs room, with its windows open towards Jerusalem. He prayed three times a day, just as he had always done, giving thanks to his God" (Daniel 6:10). Daniel knew he was disobeying the king's law, but he also knew his strength and guidance in hard times could come only from God. He would be misplacing his trust by obeying the law.

When enemies of Daniel found him praying, they told the king. King Darius had to invoke the sentence that anyone who disobeyed would be thrown into the lions' den. Daniel was facing an unknown road—the road right into the mouths of lions. Was he scared his flesh would be ripped apart and the pain would be unbearable? Did he trust God to save him as the stone was being placed over the den? This moment was the result of Daniel putting God first, and now he was facing the unknown future and it didn't look promising.

The next morning, the king hurried to the lion's den and rolled back the stone to find Daniel alive. Daniel said, "My God sent his angel to shut the lions' mouths so that they would not hurt me, for I have been found innocent in his sight" (Daniel 6:22). **Daniel's unknown road of obedience resulted in a miracle.**

In life, we will face trials that will require us to obey God and do what's right. Many times, these roads won't make sense and our ability to foresee the outcome is extremely limited, if at all. Trusting that God is greater and able to help us overcome is essential.

Over the years of my career, I was faced with telling the truth when it wasn't what leadership wanted to hear. As salespeople, we are taught to gloss over and dress up the facts, basically putting a sales spin on everything, but that practice was backfiring on the sales teams. Performance wasn't going well and leadership was demanding answers. It seems wrong to admit this, but leadership viewed the truth as an excuse, not reality. However, at this juncture I felt a conviction in my heart that I could not ignore. Lying to appease them and secure my job was wrong. I didn't know what would happen to me, I was risking being put on a written warning or worse, fired, but with much prayer and the support of a mentor, I walked the unknown road of telling the truth because it was the right thing to do. The consequences resulted in months of challenging conversations and staying true to the truth was hard. I felt worn down at times, but I hung in there. I wish I could say the situation turned around and that leadership welcomed the fresh air of truth, but that's not what happened. I ended up leaving that job on my own accord.

What right thing do you need to do? Following God and living with morals and values is sure to lead you to travel unknown roads. It might feel like you're entering the lions' den with Daniel in a culture that detests absolute truth. But trusting God will give you peace, a peace that cannot be measured or understood. It's peace from heaven. Jesus said, "I am leaving you with a gift—peace of mind and heart. And the peace I give is a gift the world cannot give. So don't be troubled or afraid" (John 14:27). The story of Daniel can inspire us with courage to obey God and faithfully travel the unknown roads of what is right.

There are so many more people in the Bible we can be inspired by, who can lift us with courage and strength to travel the unknown roads of life. Moses, Joseph, and Daniel are just a few who faced new, unexplored roadways with their eyes focused on God. They were willing to live in the unfamiliar places of life. The *Chickening IN* life is no different. The transformation journey of living with brave, bold faith will take us to unknown places. For me, I am learning to travel well. When God calls me I want to follow. I haven't always done so, but I am growing stronger, less afraid, and more willing to take risk. That is what my faith is doing in my heart, toughening me for the many roads of life.

Like I mentioned in the beginning of the chapter, traveling is a skill, and it is acquired by experience. I learned this during my time as a Strategic Sales Consultant. One to two times a month I hopped on a plane and went to a customer location or conference. My first trip was filled with anxiety and over-packing. But as I continued to travel, I learned that I had the ability to find my way in these unknown cities and unknown airports. With each trip I gained confidence for the next one.

This is what I want for you and me in our walk with Christ. Yes, walking in faith is scary, but with each step we can gain confidence in our amazing God so that the next time He asks we will be ready to follow. Traveling unknown roads is partially mustering up the guts to just do it, but there are practical things we can do to bolster our courage and strength. Tearing down the familiar is the first step. Then, positioning ourselves to catch courage by reading and studying Bible stories and learning from others who have walked brave and inspiring roads. Finally, the more we embark into the unknown the deeper our trust in God will grow, and trusting God will never fail us.

ACTION STEPS:

1. How do you handle the unfamiliar roads of life?

2. Are you afraid of the unknown or too comfy with the familiar?

3. Can you identify with any of the unknown roads we discussed?

   - Unseen and Invisible Roads

   - I Didn't Choose this Road

   - Obedience to God and Right Roads

4. Is the unknown road you are facing right now physical, spiritual, relational, or emotional?

5. What action is God calling you to today?

Learning to love yourself with all your quirks and imperfections. Refuse to be anyone but you! Let go of compassion, and embrace who God made you to be.

Chapter 6

PILLAR #5 - EMBRACING YOUR UNIQUENESS

IT'S HARD TO BELIEVE THAT Hope is entering her tween years. I've been through this twice now, but I don't think any amount of experience will prepare me to walk through the ups and downs of hormone changes, an emerging independent spirit, and the awkward social situations that are bound to arise for a third time. I'd like to think I am smarter and wiser or that somehow I won't be offended when she snaps back or pulls away. Or maybe that I can manage these next few years with confidence and the right balance of yes's and no's, and relief from the anxiety of parenting a tween by having ultimate trust in God's authority over her life.

Yes, I know I have big hopes for this roller coaster ride that comes between the ages of eight and twelve. Unquestionably, emotions will be high and low, and there will be tug-of-wars and hug-a-retreats as my daughter begins blooming from a child to a young woman. But what I'm most apprehensive about is the new awareness she will have regarding herself and others. What will she see when she looks in the mirror? How will she judge herself? Will she see the masterpiece God created with all her quirks and imperfections, embracing them because God makes no mistakes? Or will she despise those things that make her unique and special because she doesn't fit in with the secular world, the culture, or what her peers say is acceptable? Will she believe she is enough?

To be the bold, brave, faith-walking, risk-taking, traveling-down-new-roads-women-of-God we want to be, we've got to learn to embrace our uniqueness.

Have you ever struggled to believe you were enough? It was during my tween years—the same stage my daughter is in—that the battle to accept or reject myself began. It all started in fourth grade with the onset of girl drama, comparison, and catty gossip. On the playground of elementary school my self-image was being shaped and formed. New patterns of thinking established their home in the nooks and crannies of my mind, where unbeknownst to me, they would live for years. I didn't invite these negative and self-sabotaging bullies over for a playdate. They just showed up, lied to me, and I bought it. And over thirty years later these lies still drive my value and worth.

That is the great tragedy of God's daughters: not understanding the masterpiece Father God created when He carefully, delicately, and specifically created each of His women. If you're like me, then you need to go back to school and replace all those playground lies with truth and clean out the self-defeating thoughts that were set in motion so long ago. To be the bold, brave, faith-walking, risk taking, traveling-down-new-roads-women-of-God we want to be, we've got to learn to embrace our uniqueness. It is essential to the *Chickening IN* life and the next step on our journey to transform from fear-filled lives to courageous faith-filled lives.

This last year I took my daughter to the Secret Keeper Girl Masterpiece World Tour. The creator, Dannah Gresh, designed these mother/daughter sessions as warfare against the world's attack on tween girls' identity and value. The focus was on understanding what true beauty means and discovering the masterpiece God created in each girl. Sister, the message permeated my heart, and though it was intended for tweens, I could feel that nine-year-old girl inside me being ministered to and hearing life-giving words. I am a masterpiece, something nobody told me growing up.

Something I longed to hear but the world got to me first. Something that even once I became a Christian I didn't fully comprehend and something that would take years of unraveling false self-beliefs to truly believe—I am a masterpiece of God.

The Bible says, "For we are God's masterpiece. He has created us anew in Christ Jesus" (Ephesians 2:10). But what does that mean? What is a masterpiece? And more importantly, once we understand what a masterpiece is, what are the obstacles—no not obstacles, but the full-on *war* that is at work with one single goal in mind: stopping God's daughters from knowing their true value. Because if we understood our true value, we would be unstoppable ambassadors of Christ who are able to walk in faith, trust God, and love others and ourselves. We could shut down the enemy and his lies that attempt to paralyze us, and exchange deceit for rock solid truth.

What then is a masterpiece? During an interview with curators at the Louvre in Paris, home of the *Mona Lisa*, the *StarTribune*, the largest newspaper in Minnesota, asked that very question. The Parisian curators responded with "superlative craftsmanship, extraordinary design, great antiquity, rich materials, purity in form, artistic genius, and originality." It could be said that a masterpiece is an artist's greatest piece that fully embodies all their talent, skill, creativity, and workmanship at its peak.

Throughout history there have been many great artists who have produced timeless works of art: Michelangelo's Sistine Chapel, Vincent Van Gogh's *Starry Night* or Claude Monet's *Water Lilies* to name a few. These classic treasures encompass all the qualities as defined by the curators at the Louvre in Paris. But none can compare to the Master Creator—our God. By His Word the world came to be, and His work included the sky, the sea, the mountains and all creatures there within. God took nothing and made something beautiful. He is the first and original artist.

God took His artistry a step further when He created human beings. You could say we are His masterpiece above all other creation because "God created human beings in his own image" and He paid special attention to the details (Genesis 1:27). Just as an artist starts with a blank canvas or a lump of clay, God was there at the moment of conception before any form existed. He was there making the inner parts of you! The Bible says, "You made all the delicate, inner parts of my body and knit me together in my mother's womb" (Psalm 139:13). In the darkness of the womb God was creating a masterpiece, a marvelous workmanship, a unique and distinct daughter to love and be loved (Psalm 139:14-15). Stop and take that in. When you were microscopic, God was there and He was weaving a part of Himself into you—you bear the image of God.

This information is almost too amazing to believe; I am a masterpiece of God! It just doesn't make sense to me. When I look at my life, I don't see perfection or the beauty of a masterpiece. Instead I see my flaws and all the things I need to change. My weaknesses are evident, and my view of God's workmanship is limited. God can see my entire life; I see only in parts. He sees the completed picture; I see it in stages and layers. I am a work in progress, and one day when I reach Heaven I will see fully just as God sees me. Until then, in faith I must trust Him and His precious words, that I am a masterpiece of God.

In our world a masterpiece's value and worth is proven by the price someone is willing to pay for it. Not all masterpieces are equal; the more valuable and sought after, the higher the cost. Recently, my daughter and I toured a lovely local art gallery made up of a conglomerate of artists. We enjoyed seeing the talented work of local people who live near us. To purchase a piece would set us back a few thousand dollars but compare that to the value of the *Mona Lisa* at one billion dollars. The *Mona Lisa* is almost priceless. Yes, it's true the amount of money someone is willing to pay for something dictates its value. But is there another vehicle to prove value greater than money? Yes, there is . . . the exchange of one life for another. And that is the price God paid for all His masterpieces. You are worth more than the *Mona Lisa* at a shy one billion dollars because God paid for you with the life of His Son, Jesus (John 3:16). God defined your value by sacrificing His Son for you, which is of far greater worth than any amount of cash!

Did you feel your value just go up? I am wiggling in my seat right now as this revelation sinks into my heart. I am God's masterpiece and He defined my value by paying the highest price anyone can pay: giving up their life for another (1 Peter 1:18-19). But even as excited as I am in this moment, I am also very aware of the power at work against me. The world wants to define my worth and it's constantly throwing images and ideas that are contrary to God's Word. It wants me to conform and reduce my value by disliking the uniqueness God wove into the DNA that makes me, me. Satan is leading this charge and his strategy is to cause distractions that lead to identity amnesia. He wants us to forget *whose* we are by engaging us in the game of comparing.

Let's imagine for a moment that the *Mona Lisa* can see and speak. She looks around and compares herself to other masterpieces in the museum, and then suddenly recognizes she was created without eyebrows. The women in other paintings have a line of hair above their eyes that seems to accentuate their eyes and face. Are they better than her? Mona Lisa begins to doubt herself and she feels inferior. Why doesn't she have this feature that others have? She forgets that she is a one billion dollar masterpiece, and she starts complaining to her maker questioning, *why did you create me this way?* Instead of seeing her uniqueness as her maker's fingerprints on her life, she sees it as a weakness that needs to be fixed. Something she despises and wants to get rid of. She doesn't want to be unique. She wants to be like her peers. She wants to be enough.

Oh dear Sister, have you been there? Like the *Mona Lisa,* innocently observing women at church or moms at your daughter's soccer practice? Without realizing it you're comparing yourself to them. Who is a better mom or has superior children? Who has a skinnier or fitter body or is prettier? Who has a nicer car or designer clothes? This exercise leaves you feeling alone and sad. Defining your value by comparison is a no-win situation and will leave you forgetting all that you do have.

That is what comparing is like: it begins as wandering eyes trying to size up value and worth as a measuring stick against our sisters, and against the world and the culture. Insecurities are fed and the assumption that others' lives are better is enhanced. It gains momentum as the desire to change differences into likenesses increases. All the while we forget the Creator made us different on purpose, and He is pleased with His masterpiece.

Comparison crosses the line when it attacks your identity with self-defeating thoughts like *you're not good enough, you're less than, or you're not worthy to be loved or accepted.* Unhealthy comparison downplays our strengths and disables us from being who God made us to be. The Bible says our enemy is lurking around looking to devour us and he capitalizes on any opportunity to devalue us (1 Peter 5:8). He looks for weak moments to twist what was good and turn it into something harmful. If he can plant seeds of doubt about our self-worth and identity, then he can gain a foothold. Priscilla Shirer said in her book *Fervent*, "If I were your enemy I'd devalue your strengths and magnify your insecurities until they dominate how you see yourself."[10]

My first memory of defining my worth against others was in the fourth grade. A few neighborhood girlfriends and I were comparing the size of our thighs (horrifying I know, and that is why I fear for my tween daughter). My friends pointed out that my thighs were larger than theirs. I was already sensitive about my body shape, and this just added salt to the wound. Their words and my reaction would set in motion a life-long battle of body insecurity. In high school, I spent hours getting dressed because I was trying to cover up my thighs. I needed just the right combination of clothing to hide my insecurity and present the false image of skinnier legs. Everywhere I went I compared my thighs to others and I always came out on the bottom. I felt horrible about myself, and I actually believed that if anybody saw my thighs they would know the truth about me, that I was not worthy of love and acceptance.

However, my thighs weren't the only area that I experienced the dread of comparison. It's happened many times over the years, and in fact, just the other day my mind began sizing myself up against fellow Christians without my permission. It was at a women's Bible study of all places! During our small group time, we reviewed the lesson we completed the week prior, and then took turns sharing answers aloud. There are some in our group that seem well educated in Bible facts and their quick-witted answers are clever. I felt intimidated as I compared what I had written on my study guide against the wisdom being spoken in the room. My demeanor changed from excitement to discouragement. I wasn't good enough and the fear of looking stupid said, "keep your mouth shut."

Comparison was lying to me, and I had to confess my feelings to God and ask Him to renew my thoughts. The enemy Satan would like nothing more than to entrap and paralyze us. He desires ineffectiveness for the kingdom of God, and by inviting us to play the comparison game he seeks to make us forget who we are by focusing on who everyone else is. When we focus on everyone else's strengths and compare those to our weaknesses, Satan has the upper hand. We need to renew our minds in the truth of God by washing away the lies of Satan that say we're not enough, we're lacking, or we're less than, and instead pour in the truth of *who* our Creator says we are—loved, redeemed, enough, perfect in Christ, a masterpiece.

Sister, have you been entrapped by the lies of comparison? It's easy to do because our world is full of comparison traps—commercial ads, movie stars, super models and magazines are all bait that lure us to participate in unhealthy comparison, but the most powerful hook is social media. Facebook, Instagram, and other platforms are a gateway to view the "perfect" lives of our friends and family. Of course, it's only an illusion. But we forget that when we pick up our iPhone, plop on the couch, and click

comparing is a destructive habit that chips away at our identity in Christ.

the app wanting to escape from the stress of the day in our sweats, hair in a messy ponytail, make-up smeared and facial expressions that would scare a lion away, we are comparing our real world with someone else's best day. Their child just won Student of the Year, but yours is barely passing the seventh grade. They just got a new car, the one you always dreamed of, but your family is facing financial challenges and a new car isn't in the plan. She just lost fifty pounds on a new diet, but all your attempts to lose weight haven't panned out. Anytime we compare our worst to someone else's best, we will lose peace of mind and become discouraged. Christian author, Nicole Unice says, "the distraction of others' seemingly perfect life keeps us from enjoying our own."[11]

Comparing is a destructive habit that chips away at our identity in Christ. It tears down our value and worth and leads us to forget the price that was paid for our life. It spurs on discouragement and the inability to accept ourselves as God's masterpiece. But how can we break free from the enslavement of this hurtful behavior? To overcome this stronghold, we need to become secure in our identity, and by doing so we will transform our view of ourselves. Then we will find peace with our imperfections, quirks, and differences, and we will stop sabotaging ourselves with comparison.

How would you answer the question, "Who are you?"

For most of my life I believed my identity was enwrapped in how I felt. Defining my value and importance on outward circumstances and emotions has been a roller coaster ride and basing my worth on the "feelings of the day" proved to be wishy-washy. If I felt successful, courageous, and close to God, then my value went up; if I felt worried, depressed, or far from God, then my value went down. And because I have struggled with fear and anxiety, I have spent many days feeling like I am a loser or a failure. My identity roots were misplaced on the unstable, unreliable and broken foundation of emotion.

Many people answer the question of who they are with what they do: I am a doctor, I am a homeschool mom, or I am a music teacher, married with two kids. Others might look to their family of origin, nationality, or the past to describe themselves. If you get pulled over for speeding (I know that never happens), the officer will ask to see your identification which depicts your physical appearance—hair color, eye color, height, and weight. Yes, while it is true all of these things tell about you, but do they actually say who you are?

To answer the question correctly we have to have a perspective change. We need a mind shift from the external and internal circumstances and feelings to our God. We need to move away from the temptation to find value based on what we do, how we look, our past, and our emotions to *who* God says we are. What better place to understand our value and worth than to go to our Creator Himself. The Bible is clear that we are created people, and we need to look to our Creator to define us. No one else, including ourselves, is qualified for this important job and the foundation of our identity depends on getting this right.

My daughter loves to draw and paint. With each creation she describes and explains its meaning and purpose. Quite often she has a heartfelt story to accompany her artwork. The same is true for professional artists like Van Gogh, Monet, and Michelangelo. Each creator has the important task of defining their own work because they beheld the idea, vision, and final product. No one else except the designer is equipped because the creation belongs to the creator. We are created people, our Architect is God, and we belong to Him. He made us—we are His workmanship, and therefore He has the authority to tell us who we are.

Our Creator wrote us the greatest love letter of all time and within it we can find our true identity. From Genesis to Revelation, God's plan and purpose for His masterpieces is revealed. It's all written out one precious word after another. I warn you, though, there will be challenges along the way because there is a disparity between what we read and how we live it out. For example, God has redeemed us, yet we may still live like we are in bondage. However, we can confront any false beliefs and refute them with truth. God's Word is powerful. It is a weapon, a sword of the Spirit that can dispel the enemy and all his lies (Ephesians 6:17). I'd like to share ten truths and ten Scriptures that have helped me change the way I view myself:

Truth: God paid a high price for me. I am valuable.

Scripture: "For you know that God paid a ransom to save you from the empty life you inherited from your ancestors. And it was not paid with mere gold or silver, which lose their value. It was the precious blood of Christ, the sinless, spotless Lamb of God" (1 Peter 1:18-19).

Truth: I am God's child, and He is my Father. I am loved by God!

Scripture: "See how very much our Father loves us, for He allows us to be called His children, and we really are" (1 John 3:1)!

Truth: In God's economy, worth isn't based on stature, riches, or positions.

Scripture: "Who can be compared to with the Lord our God, who is enthroned on high? Far below Him are the heavens and the earth. He stoops to look, and He lifts the poor from the dirt and the needy from the garbage dump. He sets them among princes, even the princes of His own people! He gives the barren woman a home, so that she becomes a happy mother. Praise the Lord" (Psalm 113:5-9)!

Truth: God created me for a purpose. My life has meaning.

Scripture: "'For I know the plans I have for you,' says the Lord. 'They are plans for good and not for disaster, to give you a future and a hope'" (Jeremiah 29:11).

Truth: I am intimately known by God. He cares about every detail of my life.

Scripture: "O LORD, you have examined my heart and know everything about me. You know when I sit down or stand up. You know my thoughts even when I'm far away. You see me when I travel and when I rest at home. You know everything I do" (Psalm 139:1-3).

Truth: I bear the likeness of God.

Scripture: "So God created people in His own image; God patterned them after Himself!; male and female He created them" (Genesis 1:27).

Truth: I was planned by God.

Scripture: "I knew you before I formed you in your mother's womb. Before you were born I set you apart and appointed you as my spokesperson to the world" (Jeremiah 1:5).

Truth: I belong to the church, and my gifts are needed.

Scripture: "Now all of you together are Christ's body, and each of you is a separate and necessary part of it" (1 Corinthians 12:27).

Truth: I am chosen by God.

Scripture: "Long ago, even before he made the world, God loved us and chose us in Christ to be holy and without fault in his eyes" (Ephesians 1:4).

Truth: I am redeemed and forgiven.

Scripture: "He is so rich in kindness that he purchased our freedom through the blood of his Son, and our sins are forgiven" (Ephesians 1:7).

Truth: I am equipped.

Scripture: "How we praise God, the Father of our Lord Jesus Christ, who blessed us with every spiritual blessing in the heavenly realms because we belong to Christ (Ephesians 1:3).

Did your identity just strike gold? *You are chosen, you are equipped, you were planned, you are redeemed, forgiven, and known by God; you belong, you are needed, you have purpose, you have been paid for with the highest price and you are a child of God.* If we could sink our teeth into these truths and live like we believe it, we'd walk with a new bold faith able to conquer the enemy, to celebrate the strengths in our sisters without comparing, and accept our weakness as part of God's planned masterpiece. When our identity is firmly planted in God's view of ourselves, we will find peace with our imperfections, quirks, and differences.

That is what I want my daughter to know: she is a child of God. And as she walks the path from girlhood to womanhood, I pray that she sees herself as God sees her. I want her to strike gold with her identity and you, too. Yes, you

You are chosen, you are equipped, you were planned, you are redeemed, forgiven, and known by God; you belong, you are needed, you have purpose, you have been paid for with the highest price, and you are a child of God.

Sister—you are precious, loved beyond understanding, and highly desired by God. He longs for you to know your true identity.

But knowing our identity in Christ requires trust in God because our view of the final product is limited. It's like looking at the *Mona Lisa* as she was being created. The human eye couldn't see what her creator could. The human eye was limited by the physical paper, the outline sketch of her face, then the first layer of background paint, and then more color. However, Leonardo da Vinci could envision beyond what was visible. The completed picture was in his mind, and it was a matter of time before everyone else could see it, too. I wonder if during the four years it took da Vinci to paint the portrait if people questioned his talent and doubted what the final outcome would look like. I wonder if they realized they were looking at a timeless masterpiece that hundreds of years later would be priceless.

That's how it is for us. We have a narrow view of ourselves because we live a linear life according to space and time. We see only glimpses of ourselves and judge our value on a partially completed work of art. The Bible says, "Now we see things imperfectly, like puzzling reflections in a mirror, but then we will see everything with perfect clarity. All that I know now is partial and incomplete, but then I will know everything completely, just as God now knows me completely" (1 Corinthians 13:12). We must accept that we are a work in progress, and it will take our entire life to see the perfect masterpiece God has created in us. One day we will see as God sees.

Until that great day comes when we meet our maker face-to-face, it is important to trust God with every part of our lives. Celebrating our strengths is easy but accepting our weaknesses as part of the masterpiece is difficult. We want the final product now or at the bare minimum, we want a spoiler alert or to skip to the final page of the book so we know what the completed masterpiece will be. If we could foresee the future, I imagine we would welcome our shortcomings and weaknesses as an instrument helping us become the beautiful portrait God planned. But if we knew the future, we wouldn't need faith or to trust God with the outcome. Our weaknesses draw us to God and they are a vehicle for Christ's love and power to shine through us. Paul said, "Since I know it is all for Christ's good, I am quite content with my weaknesses and with insults, hardship, persecutions, and calamities. For when I am weak, then I am strong" (2 Corinthians 12:10). How do you feel about your weaknesses?

Sister, honestly I have struggled greatly with my weaknesses. As I have already shared, I am not proud of my propensity to fall prey to fear and anxiety. Many times I have suffered in silence. Shame was my master, and I felt like a bad Christian. The enemy had a field day with me, spouting accusatory, hurtful words like, *if you really believe God you wouldn't have fear. You're a poor, defeated Christian. If other believers find out they will reject you or think less of you.* Satan is so manipulative! Nothing is further from the truth, but in order to live like a masterpiece I must bring my vulnerabilities before God, confessing my fears and doubts, and allow God's love to be greater than my flaws. Like Paul, I prayed to be released from this, but God said, "My grace is all you need. My power works best in weakness" (2 Corinthians 12:9). This verse has proved true in my life. God is using my weakness to encourage others, to speak openly about fear, anxiety, and Christianity, and to literally write this book. My shortcomings are part of the masterpiece God calls me.

What weaknesses can you bring before God? Within this answer lies a testimony—a powerful story of God's grace and strength in your life. Maybe God gave you the words to speak up despite your weakness of public speaking, or maybe He strengthened you to confront a hard situation despite your weakness to have peace at all costs. Maybe He helped you take a backseat to a project because your weakness is always needing to be in control. God is glorified when we embrace our weaknesses and bring them under His authority. He covers us with mercy and grace and grows character that makes our masterpiece magnificent.

Breaking free from fear and living in faith exposes every speck of false belief, and confronting our insecurities about ourselves is part of the process. However, there is freedom awaiting us on the other side. Transforming how we think about ourselves and our weaknesses will set us up to take the next step: pursuing our dreams. God uses every part of our lives—all the pain, the grief, and the flaws as well as our strengths, talents, and gifts to set a purpose in our hearts. God's masterpieces aren't just about looking pretty, they are about fulfilling God's plan to completely develop the potential He put within you. And this is not just for yourself. It is for others to deliver the good news, to help, to advocate, to love, to give, and to encourage. Let's embrace the masterpiece that is in progress and trust God with each step along the way. Today, embrace your uniqueness as a God-given gift.

ACTION STEPS:

1. How has unhealthy comparison hurt the masterpiece God has created in you?

2. How would you answer the question, "Who are you?"

3. What Bible verse of the ten verses about your identity in Christ speaks to you the most?

4. Which weaknesses can God use to show His power in your life?

Go after your passion and calling. Don't quit pursuing your dreams. Make small steps everyday towards fulfilling your God-given purpose.

Chapter 7

PILLAR #6 - PURSUING YOUR DREAMS

THIS IS MY FAVORITE PILLAR because something magical happens when a person decides to pursue their dreams. A sparkle that was absent becomes noticeable and hope of a better future triumphs in even the most difficult of situations. It's a gift that comes filled with joy and excitement. Being able to visualize the future has the power to transform the way we live our lives. Instead of aimlessly wandering through life we can pursue fulfillment, meaning, and purpose. In Proverbs, it says that "hope deferred makes the heart sick, but when dreams come true, there is life and joy" (Proverbs 13:12). Who doesn't want that?

In chapter six, we learned that we are God's masterpiece, a unique, original, and special creation of God, and our value and worth is based on God's view of us and the price He paid for our eternal life. But He didn't create us to hang in the art gallery with *Mona Lisa*, living passively watching as others sail the seas and soar the skies. No way! He made all of us, every single one of us—yes, you—with a purpose and a plan to do the good works He intended long ago (Ephesians 2:10). That means God set a dream, a plan, and a passion within you. Our job is to uncover our God-given gifts and talents, align ourselves with God's master plan, and have the courage to take action.

I can testify that the journey to finding and pursuing my God-given dreams and purposes has transformed my heart from hopeless to hopeful. This process has increased my levels of joy. But joy didn't come easy. It's been a rough road, one I have had to fight for. One that I am still traveling. One that I have tripped and stumbled on many times. It's a process of starting, stopping, and starting again. Though not easy, I would do it all over again if I had to because I have found life, freedom, and joy beyond my wildest imagination.

How about you? Are you discovering and pursuing your dreams? Do you know what gifts and talents God gave to you? Following a dream can be terrifying. Fear is one reason we don't go after our dreams, but there are other reasons, too. Lack of knowing your purpose and passion, lack of knowing your gifts and talents, and the sobering effect of reality can all impact our ability to pursue our dreams.

One of the scariest, most butterflies-in-my-stomach producing moments of my life was the day I decided to pursue my dream. Fear was pitching a fit, but the call to follow God was stronger than the anxiety of quitting my six-figure income career. I leaped out into the unknown and started water walking with Jesus. It took years to get there. I was afraid to leave the comfort of my paycheck. I was afraid I would fail. I was afraid I was inadequate for the dream in my heart. But no matter how hard I tried to ignore it or stuff it, my dream wouldn't go away. It was a dream God planted ten years earlier and the day to abandon all fear had come—it was a *Chickening IN* moment.

It had all begun a few years earlier. I was lacking purpose and meaning in my life. Do you know that feeling? Getting up, going to work, taking care of the family, the pets, the household. Trying to accomplish this work-life balance with far too much on my plate. It seemed that days blurred into weeks and weeks blurred into months. Depression, anxiety, and moodiness took hold, while joy, excitement, and contentment declined. Asking myself some serious questions, I set out on a mission to find a meaningful life.

I had a successful career, my employer treated me well, and at times I enjoyed my work. I couldn't fathom why I was so unhappy. I was good at my job and was recognized for it many times. This really confused me and I wondered, "Is it possible to be successful at something and have no passion for it? At one time I was satisfied with my work, but not anymore—have I changed?" Regardless of the answers to these questions it was undeniable that my heart was longing for something different. In John Ortberg's book *All the Places to Go . . . How Will You Know?* he says, "Don't wait for the pain of life to force you through a door that wisdom calls you to choose now."[12] I knew it was time to take action; it was time to find and pursue my God-given dreams.

Have you ever been in that place? Life feels meaningless and every day just goes by one after another with no hope, and there is a longing for something more but you can't quite articulate what that is. Like me, maybe you question God and ask, "God what is Your purpose for my life? Please God, I am desperately seeking a meaningful life where I can make a difference and impact this world. Show me Your plan." Or maybe the discomfort is coming from God. It might be the push we need to enter a new season of life or to move towards our true calling.

Sister, I have great news for you. God answered my prayers, and I know He will answer yours, too. There is hope for all of us. The Bible says, "'For I know the plans I have for you,' says the LORD. 'They are plans for good and not for disaster, to give you a future and a hope'" (Jeremiah 29:11). The Bible is filled with encouragement to help us discover our purpose, and even better, it tells of gifts we've been given.

Since I am such a self-professed inspiration junkie, I have found that children are a sweet source of encouragement. Have you ever asked a child what she dreams of doing when she grows up? Children radiate confidence and joy in their replies, untainted by the realities of life. When my youngest daughter was four years old she aspired to be a smoothie maker and a police officer. I just couldn't help but chuckle at the contrast of those two careers, but she was self-assured this was her destiny. My heart grinned as she took my strawberry-banana smoothie order one minute and the next she pretended to arrest her teddy bear! Then I reflected on my childhood dreams. As a young girl I imagined designing beautiful gowns. My room was filled with sketches and colorings, and I visualized women, young and mature, all over the world wearing these dresses with my signature name written within them, "JJ Famous." And that just tickled me pink! What about you? What was your childhood dream—a famous singer, an Olympic gymnast, a doctor? It's so much fun to remember back when the word *impossible* didn't exist and the sky was the limit.

For an average girl from Clovis, California, I had grandiose dreams. A girl whose family life was broken, I dreamt all the more wildly with no restrictions that greater days were ahead. Days when life would be happy, content, and no longer out of control. Days when I would be in charge of my life and not hindered by the dysfunction of others. But my hopes and dreams were rudely interrupted by harsh realities. My mother died and everything changed. That once-hopeful little girl was now filled with grief, pain, and anger. My dream faded into the background and eventually died. Survival mode moved to the forefront where it would live for years, and the day-dreamy, imaginative child inside me dimmed until she no longer existed.

All these years later I found myself missing that little girl. I wanted her hopeful demeanor back. Maybe not the same dream because I had changed, but a new dream, one that only God could set within my heart. I wasn't willing to settle for anything less, and I set out on a course to find my dream—the one God planted in my heart. My journey stretches

A dream is an inner sense that I was meant to do this.

over a decade and is filled with dead ends and new beginnings, disappointments and excitement, tears and laughter. I took personality tests, spiritual gift assessments, met with a career coach, a life coach, and a counselor. I sought wisdom through Scripture, podcasts, mentors, books, and lots of prayer. Relentlessly, I pursued God and when He answered, I had to be willing to trust Him, walk in faith, and courageously pursue my dreams.

Especially in a world filled with false fairytales and ideas about what dreams are, it is important to know what a dream *is*. A dream can be described as a strongly-desired goal or purpose. It is closely tied with feelings of hope and possibility; it seems to bring meaning and fulfillment to a person's life. Often a dream won't go away and though you try to ignore it or reject it, the desire just returns. Dreams don't always make sense or match up with your ideas for life. It's like God is knocking at the door of your heart with a prompting to take action, make a change, or walk in faith. People oftentimes say, "God is calling me to . . . " A dream is an inner sense that *I was meant to do this.*

I admire people who are aware of their passions early in life. I believe that is a God-given gift. My husband was one of those people. He knew from a very early age he was meant to be a law enforcement officer, and that is exactly what he pursued and became. Somehow, I imagine that being the preferred way to know and follow dreams, but it seems more rare than common as I talk to the women in my life. Many of them aren't sure what their purpose and passion is, and like me, they have to find it. But there is hope because dreams can be realized through life experience, self-awareness, seeking God, talking with community, and trying different things. It is a process of becoming, and we can intentionally seek out and discover our dreams. That is what I had to do—I had to allow myself to imagine and dream again.

Realizing my dream started with taking a step backwards. I had to spend time getting to know myself. I knew little about who I was because I grew up in a very chaotic environment and survival was the goal. When you're trying to survive, there is little time to contemplate likes, dislikes, talents, gifts, and strengths. Maybe you struggle to know yourself, too, because an over-bearing parent told you who you had to be, or there was pressure to perform at things you didn't like. Maybe the consequences of sin kept you bound up or the fear of following your heart was too scary. Taking a time-out to get to know myself was exactly what I needed to do, and as a result I know myself better than ever.

Sister, this takes intentionality on our part. But it is an exciting process! It's like starting a new friendship with our self. In the beginning the conversation is surface level—basic things like what you prefer to eat, what hobbies you enjoy, what is your ideal job, etc. This is a great time to make a list of likes and dislikes, talents and skills, or strengths and weakness. Be detailed. Having clarity with seemingly small things will strengthen your self-awareness.

I liken this process to going into a cave and mining for gold. Darkness is all around and you're not sure where the treasure is, but as you continue to dig, God reveals a personal insight—you may have the gift of teaching, a longing to help teen moms, your heart may be to change the legacy handed to you or a new career revelation wells up. The glimmer of hope is shining bright and you're beginning to understand the direction God wants your life to go.

I experienced this glimmer of hope in 2005. My sales career started as a job to make ends meet. It wasn't my dream job, but it was provision from God. During my early years, my boss "accidentally" sent me to the wrong training class. For three days I learned from a life coach how to set goals and plan for the future. I had no idea until I returned that this class was for managers only and I wasn't a manager! However, like Proverbs 16:9

says, "We can make our plans, but the Lord determines our steps." I was sent to the training by God because it was there that He planted the seed of my dream. It all started with a question from the life coach, "Where do you envision yourself ten years from now? If you could do anything what would it be?" Temporarily, uninhibited by fear, I imagined myself encouraging women through writing and speaking. My broken past created in me a passion for women, like me, who desperately need to be told that we're good enough, lovable, and have the strength through Christ to overcome our challenges.

The life coach then asked us to write down where we would need to be in five years to achieve the ten-year goal, then two years, and we tracked it all the way back to the present day. I already subscribed to goal planning, but I had never heard it put this way before. I had always planned from the present to the future, not the future then backwards. This was revolutionary! Though my dream was big and nearly impossible from my point of view, peace came over me that day, as well as a firm acknowledgement that God was calling me to a new purpose. My current career was useful for income and learning skills for my future, but it wasn't my calling or my dream. In faith I believed that ten years later I would be released from my career and in the position of fulfilling my God-given dream.

Have you ever felt a nudge from God calling you to follow a dream or pursue a passion?

Nehemiah had a calling from God, one that God had prepared and positioned for him. It was a "for such a time as this" moment, and when the time came Nehemiah was ready to act. It started with a defining moment and a broken heart. Nehemiah just learned that Jerusalem's walls had not been rebuilt and this threatened the safety of the Jews living there. They were in great trouble. The Bible says, "When I heard this, I sat down and wept. In fact, for days I mourned, fasted, and prayed to the God of heaven" (Nehemiah 1:4).

Some dreams are born out of a defining moment when a new awareness about suffering, pain, or injustice occurs. I recall the day I first learned that sex trafficking existed. It was horrifying and it broke my heart. Or the time I realized that many unexpected pregnancies end in abortion. I know what an unexpected pregnancy feels like because I found myself in that very situation at age nineteen. My heart empathizes for young, hurting women who don't know what to do. Maybe you, too, have been deeply troubled by difficult news—that could be the beginning of a calling on your life. Think about how many nonprofit organizations were started because an average person wanted to make a difference for the hurting. I live near the headquarters for AIM (Agape International Missions). This organization began in 2005 after Don and Bridget Brewster heard about the sex trafficking problem in Cambodia. Moved by emotion, they sold their home, gave up their careers, and relocated to Cambodia to restore victimized girls and stop human trafficking.

But how can we know if our dream is from God? How can we be sure, like Nehemiah, that God is calling us? It is easy for our selfish ambitions to blind us because there is an inner battle between self-will and God's will. Knowing the difference can be difficult. Inspired from a podcast I once heard by Pastor Rick Warren, here are five questions he recommended asking yourself that will help determine if the source of your dream is God or yourself.[13] These questions made an impact on my journey and I want to share them with you.

1. DOES YOUR DREAM APPEAR TO BE IMPOSSIBLE?

If you have a dream from God, it will require God to accomplish it. If you can carry out the dream in your own power and strength, then it may not be from Him.

Consider Joseph, who as a young boy had a big dream, one his family didn't like. Quickly, he went from being the favorite son to being sold into slavery, then from Potiphar's house to prison, and finally, from prison to second-in-command to Pharaoh. Through it all, he remained faithful, and God was with him. His circumstances seemed hopeless and a lot of time passed, but his dream was a God dream, a dream only God could bring to fruition and in time what seemed impossible became reality.

If your dream seems impossible maybe that's because it is. Use wisdom and common sense when assessing your dream against this measuring stick. If my dream was to sing it would be unreasonable because I don't possess a voice that makes musical notes sound beautiful. Use sober judgement. If there is no inclination of talent, skills, or the ability to attain them it might just be a fantasy. Seek the Holy Spirit in prayer for the answer and be willing to listen. If God is calling you to it, He will help make it happen. It says in Luke that "what is impossible with people is possible with God" (Luke 18:27).

2. ARE THERE SIGNIFICANT ROADBLOCKS PREVENTING YOU FROM PURSUING YOUR DREAM?

Big dreams from God often hit major roadblocks that can make you feel discouraged, where it looks like giving up is the only option, and hopelessness threatens to take over. Imagine Moses and the Israelites as they were fleeing from Egypt. They had a dream to be freed from slavery. Running from the Egyptian army, they ran smack into the Red Sea with nowhere to go. I'm not sure about you, but that would be a showstopper for me! But God did the impossible and parted the sea so they could safely escape (Exodus 14:15-29). God performed a miracle that only He could do, and it left no room for the Israelites to take credit.

Are you facing a roadblock or dead-end? What miracles do you need to accomplish your dreams? God is the mountain-moving, water-walking, raising-the-dead-and-restoring-new-life-God of all creation. Surely He can remove your roadblock or give you the strength to go through it. Your part is to move. His part is the miracle.

3. DOES YOUR DREAM CAUSE CHUCKLING
OR LAUGHTER IN DISBELIEF?

I don't know how many times I have laughed at my dream to write. For years I struggled with a lack of confidence and I doubted my ability. Excuses filled my head, and I just thought it was a silly joke. Me? A woman with a broken past who didn't get to finish college? I kept my dream a secret because I feared judgement from others and that they would laugh or maybe even gossip about my absurd dream. Though my heart's desire was to write, I rejected it thinking it was a ludicrous longing that should be forgotten about.

That must have been how Sarah felt. She was barren, and at an age older than childbearing years, God said she would have a child. The Scripture says, "So [Sarah] laughed silently to herself" (Genesis 18:12). She longed for a child, but she had accepted it would never happen because her body was too old. The news from God that she indeed would have a child was illogical from a human perspective, but not from God's perspective.

Does your dream seem so impossible that it makes you laugh? Change your viewpoint from what is humanly possible to what is God possible. It starts with the belief that He who calls also provides. Faith in God's power is the answer. God just might turn that laughter into joy by making that dream come true. God did so for Sarah and He can do it for you. "Is anything too hard for the Lord?" (Genesis 18:14).

4. DOES YOUR DREAM REQUIRE FAITH IN ACTION?

A dream from God will require faith on your part. If you believe God, then your actions will back up your belief. Do you need to take a leap of faith and step into the unknown? Are you afraid to take action? I can't imagine how Noah felt when God asked him to build the ark—a boat nearly one and a half football fields long. It had never rained, and they were far from a body of water. Noah showed his belief in God with every piece of wood lifted and nailed together. Talk about stepping out in faith!

Is your dream on hold because you are unwilling to act? God might be waiting for you to take action, and when you do, He will show His power at work in your life. God gives the dream, but He expects us to act. What steps can you take to move toward your dream? Like Noah, start picking up your pieces of wood and begin hammering away. It might not go exactly as planned but leave no room for regrets. God is faithful and when your desire is to follow the dream He put in your heart, He will go with you.

5. DOES YOUR DREAM SERVE GOD AND HIS PURPOSES?

A final test to see if your dream is from God is to ask yourself, "Does my dream fulfill God's purpose?" Often God-given dreams serve a greater purpose—to help, heal, encourage, save, or serve others. Joseph's dream ultimately saved his family's lives. Moses' and the Israelites' dream ensured a better future for their children's children. Sarah's dream was the beginning of a great nation. Noah's dream preserved mankind and the animal kingdom. Sure, your dream will bring meaning and purpose to you personally. But look to see if it has the potential to affect someone else's life. God wants to use us for more than ourselves, our comfort, and our desires. He wants to use us to love and serve others.

These five questions are a great measuring stick to know if a dream or passion is from God, but it's equally important to spend time in prayer seeking the Holy Spirit for confirmation. The Holy Spirit is our guide and teacher and everything He says is true (1 John 2:27). He has the power to help us discern our dreams, goals, and plans to know if they are from God. It is as if the Holy Spirit ushers us into an epiphany moment, a "finally I know what direction God is leading me to go" moment. In these instants there is joy, freedom, peace, and a rising up of courage and faith to take action; a willingness to take risks because He will "equip you with all you need for doing his will" (Hebrews 13:21).

A LIFELONG CALLING

God has a universal dream for every Christian. Romans 8:29a says, "For God knew his people in advance, and He chose them to become like his Son." It is His desire that we become more and more like Christ. This is a lifelong calling that won't end until we see Christ face-to-face (1 John 3:2), and of all the dreams we have this dream supersedes them all. But it's like getting your cake and eating it, too, because as we fulfill this dream, we grow closer to Jesus and by knowing Jesus more, we discover our true selves. The more we know our true selves, the better we can understand the unique person God created us to be. And with this knowledge altogether, we can know the dreams and plans God has put within us and the special gifts and talents He wants us to use for His glory.

Remember earlier when I mentioned gifts? Well it's time to start un-wrapping! This is exciting news for all Christians because the Holy Spirit gives every person gifts (1 Corinthians 12:7). You get some, I get some . . . it's like Christmas morning! These aren't physical presents, but rather an internal gifting to equip us to accomplish God's purposes and plans for our lives, the lives of others, and the church as a whole (Ephesians 4:11-12). The first gift is for everyone who has accepted Christ as their Savior: the gift of the Holy Spirit (2 Corinthians 1:22). He is a deposit in our hearts that guarantees our salvation.

With the Holy Spirit in our hearts, He now empowers us with special abilities. Not everyone receives the same gift but every talent and ability is necessary. Not one is greater or less than another, and all are given for the purpose of serving God. Some gifts include the gift of wisdom, knowledge, faith, healing, discernment, interpretation, and prophecy (1 Corinthians 12:8-11). Other gifts are teaching, preaching, serving, encouraging, administration, giving, leading, and nurturing (Ephesians 4:11-12). We are responsible for knowing and using our gifts.

Spiritual gift tests are readily available at many churches and online, and they can help steer us in the right direction. But the best way to know your gifting is to take notice of what comes naturally and what energizes you. A great place to start is serving. There are ample opportunities to serve at church or at local nonprofit agencies, and this is a great place to practice. As

when fear won't go away, then it must go with us.

you practice in different areas of service, you may notice an ability rising up without any intention on your part. If your gift is leading you may find yourself volunteering to start a new small group or if your gift is hospitality, you may recognize that you often invite people over for coffee or dinner. Look for clues and jot them down in a notebook to reflect on and pray about. The Holy Spirit isn't trying to keep them a secret, sometimes we just need to open our eyes and see what's there.

Our spiritual gifting will often be intertwined with our dreams, purpose, and passion. That is where the magic happens, when we align our lives with God's custom design for us. This process might take time and our dreams may change as we evolve. That is why it is important to stay close to God and to allow the Holy Spirit to guide and direct our steps.

God was guiding my life those three days when my boss sent me to the wrong training. It was the beginning of understanding my deep desires, longings, gifts, and talents. My heart is for hurting women who need encouragement. I finally saw my fractured history as a gift from God to help a generation of women. I could offer my story as encouragement, wisdom, and faith that God can and will heal the damaged parts of our lives.

What talents, skills, or experiences do you have to offer to God? What gifting has He given you and how can you use that to fulfill God's purpose and plan in your life? Maybe you have discovered your dreams and know your strengths, gifts, and talents, but have not yet pulled the trigger because of fear. Fear and doubt are keeping you from pursuing your dreams. Just as quickly as faith and courage rose up and said, "I am ready to fiercely pursue my God-given dreams," fear said, "You can't. You're not good enough. People will laugh. A person with your past could never do that." The fear bully attacks. It attempts to diminish all that God is doing.

Like I mentioned at the beginning, the day I decided to pursue my dreams was one of the scariest moments of my life. Did you notice that I said *scary*? That means I was taking action *with* fear. If I waited until fear dissipated, I wouldn't be writing this book, and I wouldn't be *Chickening IN*. When fear won't go away then it must go with us.

Dear Sister, today as you are reading this, you may not be where you want to be. I know how that feels and it's okay. I don't know that we will ever completely arrive until we get to heaven. But we can make choices to move toward a better, more fulfilling life. A dear friend and career coach of mine, Coach Jen Anderson, wrote a book and coined the phrase, *Plant Yourself Where You Will Bloom*. When I think about that I picture myself digging up roots that are water deprived, ones that aren't producing fruit or foliage and transplanting them into a fertile ground. A new land that is aligned with my unique God-given gifts, talents, and interests. A place where the fruit of fulfillment, meaning, and purpose can grow. A place where peace and joy flourish. A place that, though there are challenges and it is work, the sweetness of the fruit overpowers the frustrations because that place is where I am meant to be.

Sister, don't put off pursing your dreams. I want you to bloom. That is where joy lives. You can *Chicken IN* and go after your passion and calling. It starts with taking small steps every day toward fulfilling your God-given purpose. If you don't know what your dream is, then find out. You will never regret walking in faith, following God, and trusting in Him. "Take delight in the LORD, and he will give you your heart's desires. Commit everything you do to the LORD. Trust him, and he will help you" (Psalm 37:4-5).

ACTION STEPS:

1. Are you pursuing a meaningful and passionate life?

2. Do you know what your God-given dreams and purposes are?

3. Do you know your spiritual gifting?

4. What roadblocks do you face in pursuing your dreams?

Be willing to take action regardless of fear.
Fear is an opportunity to show courage
and step in faith. Trust God and go!

Chapter 8

PILLAR #7 - DOING IT AFRAID

I SAT ON MY FOUR-WHEEL quadrunner staring at the rocky, steep mountain ahead. Fear gripped my mind and my heart beat wildly. Extreme sports is not my cup of tea, but my husband, who loves a good adrenaline rush, convinced me to go riding. I'd already faced fear along the route that day. And to my surprise it was exhilarating and empowering. But this mountain was too much. As I surveyed the situation, I tried to find the more gradual path to take, but that didn't bring any comfort because the entire mountain appeared to be a ninety-degree angle. How was I going to do it?

I attempted to go multiple times. I hit the gas as if to go, but then I'd let off and chicken out. My husband, at the top of the hill, signaled me to come up. The pressure was intense. I came to the realization that no matter what I did or how long I sat there, my concerns and worries weren't going away. I would have to do this afraid. I took a deep breath, said a prayer, and gunned it. Once I started up the hill I couldn't help but scream. I am sure every wild animal perked their ears during the sixty seconds it took for me to reach the top. I still can't believe I made it! I proved to myself that day that I can do anything if I am willing to *do it afraid*.

Sister, you can do anything, too! If you are willing to act even with angst and uneasiness in your gut, then fear will no longer be a stronghold. On my quadrunner that day when I encountered the rocky steep mountain, I had a choice to make—obey my fear or take it with me up the hill. There have been many other days I experienced the same challenges, like the day I gave notice to my boss and quit my job to pursue writing. Or the day I withdrew my daughter from public school to homeschool without having ever taught before. And I will never forget the day I didn't show up at the abortion clinic and decided to have my baby. Though my pregnancy was a surprise that terrified me, having her was the most important "doing it afraid" decision of my life. Can you remember a situation in which you did something afraid?

Grabbing hands with my fear and doing it afraid has been a learning process, an area of growth that is still in development, and the reason that I am obsessed with courage. *Chickening IN* has been God's way of teaching me, and I love what God is doing.

Up until this point we have learned ways to lay down fears and defeat our worries. We have become strategic thinkers, mindful of God's love for us, and the unique plan He has for each of us. Now we are turning a corner on our journey and instead of trying to rid ourselves of fear we are going to embrace it. This is the pillar of guts, grit, nerve, and backbone. I have learned the hard way, sometimes fear is here to stay and doing it afraid is necessary. This is the next step to transforming our fear-filled lives into courageous, faith-filled lives.

The word *courage* has often perplexed me. At face value I assumed that to have courage is to have no fear, but nothing could be further from the truth. The very definition of courage implies that fear is present—it's the mental or moral strength to venture, persevere, and withstand danger. There would be no need for courage if feeling afraid didn't happen. In fact, courage cannot exist in the presence of fearlessness, and without feelings of uneasiness and insecurity, courage would become extinct.

The truth is that since the Garden, mankind has struggled with being afraid. Three chapters into Genesis, Adam and Eve hid from God

> This is the pillar of guts, grit, nerve, and backbone.

because they were afraid (Genesis 3:10). Fear's attack hasn't stopped since, and no one is immune from it. We have a limited perspective on life, and there's only so much we can do to alleviate the feelings of fear. Even with all our efforts to conquer fear and trust God, we can still feel afraid. That feeling can become a showstopper, causing us to refuse to move forward. The misconception that fear and doubt must be absent to take action is not true, and yet we still find ourselves longing for a fear-free life.

Is it realistic to believe that we will always perfectly respond to the unknown and ever-changing circumstances of life? Absolutely not. As it is, most of us can recall numerous situations that fear refused to exit our lives. I like to call these moments "courage opportunities" or times when we can prove our faith and trust in God by taking action though we feel frightened.

History proves that greatness comes when people are willing to do it afraid. Surely the Wright Brothers harbored fearful emotions as they set flight for the first time. Or what about Neil Armstrong—how many butterflies do you think were in his stomach when he launched off to the moon? What about Rosa Parks sitting on the bus refusing to move from her seat? She must have been shaking on the inside, but that didn't stop her from taking action. She said, "I have learned over the years that when one's mind is made up, this diminishes fear."[14] Throughout history, it's people who were willing to do it afraid that ushered in change, accomplished the impossible, and did more than they ever dreamed. Feeling fearful didn't stop their courageous action.

Doing it afraid is no easy task. While I prefer predictable outcomes, walking in faith hardly ever offers that. Maybe God is more interested in growing my trust in Him instead of making me so comfy that I forget what He's done for me. In my life I have noticed three areas of growth that have helped me walk forward regardless of fear's invasion. These areas have been battled out in my mind over and over again, challenging my need for control and redefining my idea of courage.

1. ONLY GOD KNOWS THE OUTCOME

Hebrews' Hall of Faith records numerous accounts of people who willingly followed God without knowing exactly how it would turn out (Hebrews 11). They went by faith and left the results to God. I can't imagine the fear Noah might have felt as he assembled the ark (Hebrews 11:7), or the terror Abraham experienced as he led Isaac up the mountain (Hebrews 11:17). I wonder if Moses' parents felt uneasy during the three months they hid their baby boy from the king (Hebrews 11:23). We could go on and on about people who followed God faithfully and courageously, yet they didn't let fear stop them nor did they demand that God reveal the final outcome. They had a confidence in God that outweighed the unknown future.

How can we be like Noah, Abraham, Moses, and so many others in the Bible? How can we have peace with the unknown outcomes of our faith decisions? There are two truths about God that have given me the initiative to proceed regardless of my fearful emotions. My ability to do it afraid has been transformed by placing these truths deep within my heart and remembering them frequently: God guides me and God goes before me.

> "Your own ears will hear him. Right behind you a voice will say, 'This is the way you should go,' whether to the right or to the left" (Isaiah 30:21).

The future can be scary and not knowing how it will turn out causes more fear. On my own I have good reason to be scared. But when I seek God, I can rest assured He is leading and guiding me into my future. When I turn my attention to Him, He provides wisdom, discernment, and direction. He will not hold back on giving me the courage I need to take each next step. I am thankful that I can be confident in God's guidance for my future, and because of that I can move forward trusting Him. I can do my part by obeying and going, and then trusting Him to lead me in whatever may come.

> "You see me when I travel and when I rest at home. You know everything I do . . . You go before me and follow me. You place your hand of blessing on my head" (Psalm 139:3, 5).

God is everywhere and He exists outside of space and time. He sees our entire life from beginning to end. This is hard for the human brain to comprehend. Because God is omnipresent (Psalm 139:7), He goes before us and He prepares us for what is to come. I have experienced great comfort in "doing it afraid" knowing that God goes before me. Because He knows what is to come, He is qualified to lead and guide me. When difficult situations arise, I repeat this motto, "God knew this was coming and because He knew it, He has prepared me in advance to walk through it." I am thankful that when I am afraid, I can still follow God because He is paving the way.

Our deep desire to know the future is pointless. There's no foreknowledge of the outcome for all our courageous decisions. However, we can be assured that God guides us and God prepares us. And when we look to God to help us persevere through our fears, we can be sure He will answer. He can set us free by giving us the ability to trust in Him and do it afraid.

2. MORE CONFIRMATION ISN'T THE ANSWER

Some of the biggest decisions of our lives can cause us to want to check and double check that it is the right choice. Changing jobs, moving to a new city, starting a ministry, or deciding to get married bring up the need for "more confirmation" than is necessary. Fear of making a mistake can delay the decision or lead to indecision. If we have already well-considered the plan, then desiring more confirmation might be an excuse to play it safe.

Gideon was a man called by God to rescue the Israelites from the Midianites (Judges 6:14). He was blinded by his limitations and doubted his ability deferring to his social status as the least in the family (Judges 6:15). Though an angel appeared to Gideon and answered Gideon's request for a sign, it still wasn't enough (Judges 6:17-22). Gideon asked for two more miracles to confirm that he should act (Judges 6:37-39).

I don't know how many times I have said to someone, "If God gave me a sign then I wouldn't be afraid to make this decision." Earlier in the book I shared a story about a nonprofit job that I regret turning down. I, too, asked God for signs. Graciously, God provided one after another confirming that this job was His will, but no amount of signs could take away the fear I felt. More confirmation wasn't going to calm my fears or make me able to act. I already had everything I needed to make the choice except the faith to say yes.

Maybe you, too, have had similar thoughts: *If only God would spell it out, give me proof, or come down from Heaven and speak directly to me then I would.* Sure, it's wise to collect all the facts before taking a risk but demanding that God give signs can be a form of unbelief. The Pharisees asked Jesus for a sign to prove that He was from God (Matthew 12:38). They had seen plenty of signs and wonders, but their hearts refused to believe. Jesus knew they had a wealth of evidence and that more miracles wouldn't make a difference, so He denied their request (Matthew 12:39).

Fear can create a never-ending cycle of requiring one more sign from God. In this life we can never be completely sure. We have to take chances and try. But we have something Gideon didn't have—we have an instruction manual, the complete revealed Word of God. Paul reminds us, "All Scripture is inspired by God and is useful to teach us what is true and to make us realize what is wrong in our lives. It corrects us when we are wrong and teaches us to do what is right. God uses it to prepare and equip his people to do every good work" (2 Timothy 3:16-17). Instead of demanding signs and miracles we need to rely on God's Word to direct our path. By spending time studying the Scriptures we can gain insight into God's will for our lives, and once we know the truth, there is no need for additional confirmation. It's just a matter of making the decision to do it afraid.

We can learn to be satisfied with the still, small voice within us telling us to go this way or that way. Though we are afraid and would prefer more confirmation, we can move forward because God is trustworthy. Knowing that God guides us brings reassurance that if we start down the wrong path

He will redirect our steps. Confidence in God's ultimate authority over our lives will help us overcome needing more confirmation.

3. REVERSING THE "WHAT IF" SYNDROME

Sister, please tell me I am not the only one who struggles with What-If. She is similar to the fear bully because she wants us to stay in our comfort zones. Her goal is to make a claim in our hearts by whispering lies that feed our deepest fears. More than anything, she wants things to remain the same and she will scare us into complacency. What-If is no respecter of persons and she knows just what to say to shrink our courage. You might be familiar with some of her questions: *What if I fail? What if I am not good enough or smart enough? What if I am just a dreamer and my dreams are too big to be fulfilled? What if they reject my ideas and I look like a fool? What if no one believes in me and I am all alone?*

What-If craves safety and sameness. Walking in faith is too uncertain for her. She loves staying within her four walls. Left unattended, she can cause us to refuse to walk in faith, trust God, and make courageous choices. And we might miss out on our destiny one fearful thought at a time. When we refuse to act, What-If wins and her presence in our heart grows stronger. By buying into her lies and giving into fear we cut God out of our life. Instead of walking boldly and bravely with God we end up deferring to a life of no growth, no healing, no adventure, and no change.

In the Scriptures, we are reminded that "God has not given us a spirit of fear and timidity" (2 Timothy 1:7). In addition, we are instructed to take our false thoughts captive and view them in light of God's truth (2 Corinthians 10:5). What-If lies to us all the time, but what if we take her captive and view What-If from another perspective? What if we let God use What-If to propel us to greater courage and faith? After all, Scripture says that what Satan meant for harm God meant for good.

It is simple: we need to reverse What-If. Just a slight shift in aligning our perspective with God's would look something like this: *What if I don't take this chance and I miss out on God's will for my life? What if I stay complacent and reach the end of my life regretting that I never followed my dreams? What if my ideas could have impacted the world and people for good, but I never took the risk? What if I live the rest of my life with this pain and I never grow? What if I never walk in faith and give God the chance to do only what He can do?*

Today, what will you do with What-If? Will you continue to entertain her lies or will you take your thoughts captive and allow God to transform you? God promises to be with you and me. When facing What-If, ask yourself this question: *On my last day here on earth, will I regret chickening out, playing it safe, and not doing it afraid?* Have courage, my friend, for God says, "This is my command—be strong and courageous. Do not be afraid or discouraged. For the LORD your God is with you wherever you go" (Joshua 1:9).

LEARNING FROM GIDEON

These three areas of growth will help prepare us to do it afraid. However, even with all the preparation, it still might not be enough to say yes to that scary decision, taking that risk, or walking in faith. John Ortberg says, "If you wait to move until you're finally ready, you'll wait until you die."[15] I don't want you or me to die having regretted not venturing out to see what is on the other side of fear. God has plans for our lives and waiting for perfect circumstances and perfect feelings to act might delay the good things He has in store for us.

When we look to the Bible, we can see many people, like us, who had to do it afraid. One example is Gideon, who had less than perfect circumstances. Gideon was preparing his army of 32,000 to rescue the Israelites from 135,000 Midianites, and the Bible says, "The Lord said to Gideon, 'You have too many warriors with you'" and God instructed him to reduce his army down to 300 (Judges 7:2). I am not in the military, but watching soldiers leave the battlefield would cause a surge of fear to rise within me, and I would doubt the circumstances and my ability to be successful. I have felt that way in my life too—times when the task ahead looked impossible. Like David staring up at Goliath, my little pebbles stacked up against a mighty giant. I bet you have endured times like these, and they can be discouraging.

Gideon was afraid, but his fear didn't erase God's calling. God in all His goodness provided a boost of courage. The Bible says, "But if you are afraid to attack, go down to the camp with your servant Purah. Listen to what the Midianites are saying, and you will be greatly encouraged" (Judges 7:10-11). Gideon did as God directed. In his obedience Gideon overheard a man describing a dream that meant God had given victory to Gideon (Judges 7:14), and he was strengthened to move ahead. God understands our fears, and we can experience encouragement just like Gideon did when we listen and obey God first. Whatever battles you are facing today, know that God wants to equip you to do that scary thing.

Sister, I don't know what frightening situation is standing before you. Maybe it's a looming marital problem or a broken friendship. Maybe it's the need to look for a job or change your child's school due to unfortunate circumstances. Maybe it's a struggle with anxiety because life is overwhelming right now and everything you attempt to do feels uneasy. It might look scary from our point of view, but nothing, no matter how intimidating, is too scary from God's view.

> **It might look scary from our point of view, but nothing, no matter how intimidating, is too scary from God's view.**

We can do it afraid when we trade our fears, apprehensions, and concerns for faith and trust in God. The Bible says, "He alone is my refuge, my place of safety; he is my God, and I trust him" (Psalm 91:2). By turning to God in our despair and finding shelter in His arms, He will strengthen us to move in faith, and our faith will grow. Sarah Young said in *Jesus Calling*, "I am continually with you, so don't be intimidated by fear. Though it stalks you, it cannot harm you, as long as you cling to my hand."[16] Such a beautiful picture of a daughter tightly gripping the hand of her father.

And that leads us to our final thought. Have you ever noticed that children are able to do it afraid when they are with their daddy? I've watched all three of my daughters face fears over and over again because my husband has the ability to talk them through it. He knows what they are capable of and he expects them to rise up to their potential. He doesn't allow them to wimp out or take the easy road of giving up. I have witnessed my daughters do things they didn't think were possible because their daddy is strong and he believes in them. They knew they could trust him with their life.

Hope struggles with the fear of change and the fear of new situations. She prefers everything to remain the same, but that causes many challenges because life is always changing. The first time we went to Six Flags my daughter reacted anxiously. The loud noises of the roller coasters and the crowds caused an uneasiness and she wanted to go home. However, David lovingly grabbed her hand and led her into the park. He promised to stay with Hope and even go on a few kiddie rides. His presence gave her strength to proceed in the midst of her worry and doubt. As the day went on fear slowly began to disappear, and when it was time to go home, she begged us to stay!

Sister, we have a Heavenly Father who believes in us, too, and our Father is the strongest, most powerful King in all the universe. He spoke the world into existence (Psalm 33:9). He knows everything about us (Psalm 139:1). He also knows our potential because He created us with a plan and a purpose (Jeremiah 29:11). When hard and scary times come, and they will, our Father is right beside us guiding us with His Word (Psalm 16:8; 119:105), and in our Father's strength we can scale walls, climb mountains, and cross the seas of life (Psalm 18:29). Fear may come, but it doesn't intimidate Him. When we focus on our Father, we can do anything He is calling us to do.

when we are willing to do what we are afraid of, we become unstoppable daughters of God.

On this side of Heaven, fear will always be a factor. Life is ever changing, and because we have limited vision, we are susceptible to fear's attack. However, our fearful emotions don't have to control our ability to move. With faith and trust in the One who is greater, our Father, we can feel afraid and act anyway. We can grab our fear by the hand and take it with us. And when we are willing to do what we are afraid of, we become unstoppable daughters of God.

My dear sister, do it afraid.

ACTION STEPS:

1. What situation are you facing right now in which you need to just "do it afraid?"

2. Which of the growth areas do you struggle with the most?

3. Can you take one tiny, brave step today to begin to build your courage muscle?

4. Knowing who your "Heavenly Father" is, how does this help you "do it afraid?"

Leaning on and trusting God with every step of the journey. Drawing close to Him and seeking His Word. Believe. Hope. Pray.

Chapter 9

PILLAR #8 – FAITH THE DIFFERENCE MAKER

I HAVE NEVER BEEN MUCH of a cook, but I do enjoy baking, and because I love bananas I've become obsessed with making the perfect banana bread. Endlessly I have worked to add and remove ingredients to find the impeccable combination that makes everyone's taste buds go bananas! On one occasion, I guess I was overly excited because I left out a core ingredient. I didn't realize it until I took my bread out of the oven and noticed that it was flat. I had forgotten to add the eggs.

The banana bread was edible, but without eggs it didn't reach its full potential because eggs are a critical component. They supply nutrition, color, and flavor, but most importantly they provide structure for stickiness and a leaven effect to make the dough rise. While each ingredient has a purpose and necessity, the eggs are the glue that makes it all come together. That is how the final pillar of *Chickening IN* is—Faith is the Difference Maker, the adhesive that holds all the other pillars together and allows us to reach our full God-given potential.

So far on our *Chickening IN* journey, we have learned about seven of the key ingredients to transform our fear-filled lives into courageous faith-filled lives. The final and most important additive to our formula is faith. Faith is as essential to *Chickening IN* as eggs are to my banana bread recipe. With faith you'll travel further, climb higher, and swim deeper. Faith is the difference between temporary or lasting change. I like to call it the icing on the cake and the frosting between the layers.

I want to clarify right from the beginning that faith is a complicated word to define. This chapter isn't a theological debate about the many ways faith can be explained, but rather it's about the power of faith in our everyday lives. It's the belief that God can do the impossible not just for the people in the Bible, the missionaries overseas, or the neighbors across the street, but for us, too. With His help, we can overcome our deepest fears, walk with newfound courage and strength, and tell our mountains to move and they will (Matthew 17:20). When we put full confidence in God, He won't disappoint us. Faith is the difference maker because faith is knowing that God, though invisible, is with us, guiding and leading us to become the brave women He planned us to be.

I've only begun to experience the power of walking in faith. For years I struggled to move my faith from my head to my feet. Fearfulness and anxiety have been a stronghold for me, and though I am a Christian I haven't always experienced victory over my past, my pain, or my sin. The majority of the battle has been waged in my thoughts. Honestly, I doubted that God would work miracles in my life. I believed He did for others, but not for me and that caused me to have cautious faith—faith that wanted proof. The areas of my life that needed transformation had no visible solutions. When I decided to move my feet in faith, it provided an opportunity for God to show me that He wants to do miracles in my life, too.

Sister, what story of faith do your feet tell? Do they speak of the wear and tear of walking the narrow, steep path of faith or are they rarely in use because your faith walk is weak or nonexistent? Walking in faith can be difficult because it goes against our worldly instincts of self-preservation, need for control, and fear. But, without faith, it will be difficult to become the courageous, brave women of God that He is calling us to be. *Chickening IN* on our own has limitations that keep us from experiencing victory over fear. Trying to see beyond the visible world into what is possible with God is impossible without faith. Faith then is the channel by which God's power is manifested in our lives.

> Faith then is the channel by which God's power is manifested in our lives.

What does it mean that, by faith, God's power is made real in our lives? How exactly does it enhance or increase our ability to transform fear into courage?

Over the years of my battle to overcome fear, I have come to learn about four principles of faith that are at work in my life. These principles have helped me to tangibly see how faith makes a difference. Just like the eggs that gave my banana bread structure, these four principles provide the framework for how faith makes a difference in our ability to transform from fear to courageous faith.

FAITH GIVES US THE POWER TO ACT

When I was about ten years old, my father picked me up for dinner. It was a weeknight and not our normal every other weekend visit. During our few hours together, we got into a discussion about how many states there were in America. In school we were studying the states and I told my father I had learned there were fifty-two of them, Alaska and Hawaii being the last two. My father disagreed because he believed there were fifty states, and we began to debate. Both of our beliefs were so strong that we bet five dollars and shook on it. Back then we didn't have smartphones to look it up on the spot, so we couldn't announce the winner until I went back to school the next day and asked my teacher. To my surprise my father was right. I share this story with you because it's one of those memories that, after thirty or so years, is still clear as day, and although I was wrong it illustrates the point well—the conviction of our beliefs will cause us to take action.

There are many men and women in the Bible who took action based on their belief in God, and their willingness to stick their neck out for what they regarded as truth was proven by their steps. Faith in God propelled them to action. By faith Noah built the ark, Abraham left his home in search of a new land, and Moses led the Israelites out of slavery. The Bible says that faith is, "The confident assurance that what we hope for is going to happen. It is the evidence of things we cannot yet see" (Hebrews 11:1).

When we believe that what we hope for will happen, it changes how we behave. The Bible says, "What's the use of saying you have faith if you don't prove it by your actions?" (James 2:14). True faith doesn't just reside in our intellectual mind, but it's demonstrated by behavior. For example, if you believe it is going to rain you will take your umbrella. The umbrella is proof that you think it will rain. Faith gives us the power to act because it transforms what we believe into what we do.

I often think of Peter and the moment his legs went over the edge of the boat and his feet touched the water. His confidence that Jesus had the power to keep him from sinking was evident by his actions. If Peter didn't act, he never would have experienced walking on water with Jesus. The ability to overcome any fears and doubts about the laws of gravity didn't come from within himself. His hope had to be in something or Someone greater than himself and more powerful than the waves. It was Peter's faith in Jesus that gave him the courage to go.

Faith has activated my feet many times. Every step I have taken is because I believed God was with me, empowering, leading and guiding my every step. Last year my daughter and I desired to be part of a mother daughter group for tween aged girls. We couldn't find one that met our needs and I felt a nudge from God to start a group. By faith, I took action first by praying, then seeking confirmation from others. When I felt confident that God wanted me to proceed, by faith, I began the administrative process of picking a start date, a Bible study book, and sending out invites.

> Faith will engage our feet when our belief is not in our strength, but in God Almighty's.

By faith a wonderful group was assembled, and we just recently completed our second Bible study and now we are gearing up for our third.

How has faith mobilized your feet? What amazing stories would you tell me if we were sitting together having coffee? Maybe you'd share times when you didn't walk in faith but halted because of fear and doubt. It's happened to me, too. Remember we are on a journey and we will stumble at times, but God is gracious and patient. Like Peter, when we place our trust in the One who is greater than any circumstance we could ever endure, our faith will empower us to walk on the water of our problem or situation. Faith will engage our feet when our belief is not in our strength, but in God Almighty's.

FAITH WILL TAKE US FURTHER THAN IMAGINABLE

On our own, we have the capacity to make things happen. Because we are made in the image of God we have the ability to plan, foresee, and operate (Genesis 1:27). However, our capabilities are restricted to the visible world. Without God we are limited. Without faith we will never reach our potential or experience God's amazing miracles in our lives and the lives of others.

I love this story in the Old Testament in 2 Kings. It's about a widow stuck in a situation that, on her own, she couldn't overcome. Her resources were depleted, her ability to make things happen reached its limit, and she could not foresee how the future would work out for good. This poor widow had one flask of oil and that wasn't enough to cover her debt. She was scared because the creditors threatened to take her two sons as slaves to satisfy what she owed (2 Kings 4:1). The widow approached the prophet Elisha for help. Elisha asked the widow, "Tell me, what do you have in the house" (2 Kings 4:2)? She replied that she had nothing except the flask of olive oil. Elisha instructed her to borrow as many empty jars as she could, and then go and pour the oil from her flask into all the empty containers. Every jar was filled to the brim until the last one, and then the oil stopped flowing. The widow was able to sell the jars of oil to pay off her debt with plenty left over to support her family.

The widow's faith in action took her much further than she could have ever gone on her own. She had limited resources, but God's resources are limitless. What was impossible for the widow was possible with God (Matthew 19:26). Her faith to obey Elisha by gathering the jars and pouring the oil from the single flask into the empty jars resulted in God's abundant provision. Faith took her further than she could have ever imagined.

As an adult, I dreamed of a life free from the negative triggers of my childhood and early adulthood pain. I believed I wasn't lovable enough or good enough, and when others showed disappointment in me or failed to acknowledge that I was good, I spiraled downward. On my own I tried to will my thoughts to change and I even tried to forget them altogether. I had some success, but it didn't last, and eventually it resulted in anxiety and depression. It wasn't until faith took front and center that I was able to make progress. My emotional healing didn't come overnight. It has been a gradual process of acting in faith. By faith I went to counseling. By faith I started studying the Bible and have been for over twenty-four years now. By faith I accepted God as my ultimate authority. By faith I know I will never be perfect, but I am perfectly loved by Him. By faith I forgave the people who hurt me. I am in a new emotional place that wasn't possible on my own. God's love has desensitized my heart from the triggers of the past. My faith has taken me so much further than I ever have dreamed possible, and there is still more to come.

How about you, Sweet Sister? Are you walking in faith or in your own strength? When God's mighty power is at work within us, we will be amazed at what He can and will do (Ephesians 3:20). God is able to do infinitely more than we could ever imagine. Faith will take us further on our journey to heal from the past, to overcome our fears and doubts, and to pursue a life filled with purpose and meaning. Faith will give us courage we cannot muster up on our own—the kind of courage that gathers empty jars and tilts the flask with the hopeful assurance that God will provide.

FAITH WILL KEEP US GOING WHEN IT LOOKS IMPOSSIBLE

Have you ever watched American Ninja Warrior? Brave men and women attempt to complete one athletic obstacle after another. Each section of the course is extremely challenging and finishing is nearly impossible. Very few make it to the finals, if anyone at all, but every year the competitors keep coming back. Relentlessly competitors train with the hope of making the impossible possible. They dream of making it, and Mount Midoriyama keeps them motivated even when it appears out of reach, but for the Christian, faith is what keeps us going.

The ability to tackle the impossible situations of life is only imaginable with faith. The Bible reminds us of many faith walkers who faced insurmountable circumstances. How could Daniel be willing to walk into the lions' den or Shadrach, Meshach, and Abednego be willing to step into the fire? Death appeared to be the only probable outcome

> The ability to tackle the impossible situations of life is only imaginable with faith.

for all, and yet they were ready to follow God anywhere, everywhere, and anytime. In this hopeless situation how were they able to fearlessly and courageously proceed?

Though Shadrach, Meshach, and Abednego were offered a choice by Nebuchadnezzar to either bow down to him or be thrown into the fire, they refused to dishonor God. They said, "If we are thrown into the blazing furnace, the God whom we serve is able to save us. He will rescue us from your power, Your Majesty. But even if he doesn't, we want to make it clear to you, Your Majesty, that we will never serve your gods or worship the gold statue you have set up" (Daniel 3:16-18). These three men had faith that God could rescue them, and they were determined to remain faithful to Him regardless of the outcome. Yes, the situation looked hopeless, but it was their confident assurance in God that kept them going.

A major turning point in the ability of our faith to keep us going in impossible situations is to let go of the outcome. Shadrach, Meshach, and Abednego were willing to accept the consequences no matter what happened. They were thrown into the fire, but something amazing occurred. Nebuchadnezzar and his advisors expected to see three burning bodies, but instead they saw four figures walking around the fire untouched by the flames. The Scripture says, "The fourth looks like a god" (Daniel 3:25)! God sent a supernatural being or maybe even Christ Himself to be with them during their impossible situation. Completely untouched by the fire, Shadrach, Meshach, and Abednego were delivered that day. I am sure they never imagined how it would work out, but their faith in God caused them to persevere during the most difficult of times. Their faith kept them going.

Do you find it hard to trust God with the outcomes of impossible situations? When we trust God to either deliver us here on earth or in Heaven, we remove the constraints of control. By allowing God to be in control of how it turns out we open ourselves up to unimaginable possibilities. Shadrach, Meshach, and Abednego got to walk in the fire unharmed with one sent from Heaven. I wonder how many miracles I have missed out on because I didn't let my faith keep me going when I couldn't see beyond the flames. The nonprofit job I didn't take—it's true I couldn't see beyond the fiery roadblocks that appeared to be impossible to put out. If I had let my faith lead, I wonder how God might have brought extraordinary solutions to my impossible situation.

FAITH STRENGTHENS OUR BELIEF IN GOD

My first day at work as a sales professional I remember feeling insecure and unsure of myself. I hadn't worked outside of the home for several years and I felt out of place. Quickly I had to learn the material and be ready to give a sales pitch to potential business clients. At first it was awkward, and I stumbled when delivering the presentation. However, as I continued to meet with customers my confidence grew, and the more I spoke about the products and services the more it reinforced my understanding of them.

My faith has been somewhat like my sales career. The more I do it, the more confident I grow to continue doing it. Another way to put it is that every time I step out in faith, the more faith I grow in God. Without living in faith, my faith has little chance of compounding. Just like my knowledge of the sales material, if I didn't go out and present, I would never get better at presenting. Think about Abraham. He didn't just walk in faith one time. Over and over again he boldly followed and trusted God. Abraham moved to a new land, lived like a foreigner, had a child together with Sarah at an older age, and then—maybe his biggest step of faith of all—he walked Isaac up the mountain as a sacrifice. Every time Abraham affirmed his trust in God by acting in faith, it reaffirmed how trustworthy God really is, and every step was preparing him for the next. When we live in faith it strengthens our belief in God.

I have noticed this principle at work in my life. Walking in faith has been a doing it afraid action for me. Every time I choose to trust God and ignore my fear, my belief that God can be trusted grows. This has been the most gratifying part of walking in faith. Being in a relationship with God and seeing how He lovingly responds to my faith steps has just made Him more real to me. How about you? Have you recognized your belief in God gaining momentum when you step out in faith? For one reason or another you may have said to someone, "You don't know what you're missing." If we are not walking in faith, then we don't know what we are missing either. Faith is an opportunity to strengthen our relationship and belief in God.

These four principles have taken the invisible and made it tangible to me. I can see God's power at work in the details of my life. The Bible says that faith is, "The confident assurance that what we hope for is going to happen. It is the evidence of things we cannot yet see" (Hebrews 11:1). Faith knows that God is with us, helping us even though we cannot physically see Him; He is there. We gain strength over this world when we go in faith because God is the foundation of our faith, and He has overcome this world (John 16:33).

God is pleased when we display the fruit of faith in our lives (Hebrews 11:6). Faith becomes the conduit that God accomplishes for us what we cannot do ourselves. However, we must be careful that faith doesn't become a grocery list of things we want. John Ortberg says, "Faith is not about me getting what I want in my outer world; it's about God getting what He wants in my inner world."[17] True faith will always result in a changed heart and character growth. It's not about the outer world: God is most interested in our inner world.

We must be careful not to confuse feelings for faith or faith for feelings. I've been guilty of this myself. Many times I believed I could not act in faith because I did not feel inspired, strong, or spiritual enough. Several years ago I missed out on an opportunity to lead a women's Bible study because I felt weak. My marriage was going through a valley, and I thought I had to have it all together. Instead of trusting God's leading and moving in faith I declined the offer. Feelings do not dictate faith. Truth does that, and when truth is the foundation of our faith we move regardless of how we feel.

Since fear is a very strong emotion, faith becomes a critical ingredient to a transformed life. Like the frosting between the layers of cake, so should faith be layered throughout our *Chickening IN* journey. When it

When we refuse to let the emotion of fear guide our path, faith has a chance to make a difference in the movement of our feet.

comes to facing our fears, faith is the difference between being stuck in despair or experiencing triumph. On our own, our fears and doubts can consume us. Without warning, worries and anxieties can suddenly attack, causing us to take our eyes off Jesus. It's like the disciples out in the middle of the lake when the unexpected storm arose (Matthew 8:23-27). As the waves came crashing into the boat, they forgot all the miracles Jesus had previously performed. Though Jesus lay sleeping just a few feet away from them, they began weathering the storm in their own strength. They traded faith for fear. However, once they realized the storm was too powerful they called out, "Lord, save us! We're going to drown" (Matthew 8:25)! Immediately Jesus awoke and calmed the storm.

Sister, I wish I could understand the human heart. Why do we continually forget the power of God over the storms in our lives? I know from my own experience that fear and doubt are powerful emotions. Maybe that's why the Bible is constantly reminding us to recount what God has done for us (Psalm 40:5), because God knows how easily we are distracted by what we see and what we feel. Like the disciples, fear can sabotage our faith and when we feel afraid, it can cause us to forget to call upon the name of Jesus.

However, I just love this—did you notice how quickly Jesus responded to the disciples? All it took was *one* call. That is the difference faith makes when facing our fears. Faith says, "Jesus, I need Your help." Faith says, "God is greater than this fear, doubt, or worry." Faith says, "The same power that calmed the storm is living with me." When we focus on God our fears shrink back, and that makes room for God's power to overcome the storms in our life.

When we refuse to let the emotion of fear guide our path, faith has a chance to make a difference in the movement of our feet. Life is a series of challenging situations that present a choice to step up to the plate of our life and obey what God is calling us to do or cower back in fear. Though the situation—like financial hardship or a broken marriage—seems like a giant wall blocking our pathway, God is asking us to start climbing. Faith becomes an act of obedience.

I think about Joshua and the Israelites as they stood before the wall of Jericho, an enormous barrier that, in some places, stood over twenty-five feet tall and twenty feet thick. God told Joshua that Jericho was already delivered to him (Joshua 6:2), but first they had to obey God's directions. In faith that God would do what He promised, the Israelites had to step up and march around the city seven times. The seventh time around they shouted loudly and the walls of Jericho came tumbling down (Joshua 6:20). Imagine if they refused to step up to the plate and march—it could have changed the entire course of history. Faith made the difference that day.

By marching around Jericho, Joshua and the Israelites were confirming their faith in God's promise. Though they could not see their deliverance they believed God, and their confidence in Him caused their feet to move. Sister, if God can tear down a physical wall like Jericho, He can surely break down the walls and barriers in your personal life. But we must be willing to carry out His directions. Sometimes that might be obeying Scripture, and other times it might be an inner conviction brought on by the Holy Spirit. In either case, having the faith to step up to the plate of your life and move your feet in obedience is the difference between victory or defeat.

Faith is built upon truth and obedience to God, and it is never reckless. When taking courageous risks, faith isn't propelling into the unknown without preparation. That is irresponsible. Rather, faith makes a difference by taking calculated risks. The Bibles says, "Don't lose sight of good planning and insight" and "the prudent carefully consider their steps" (Proverbs 3:21, 14:15). Faith isn't the abandonment of common sense or wisdom, but rather incorporating them into your risk strategy. Since risk inherently means no guarantee, faith then becomes the vehicle by which, after all planning is done, action is set in motion.

Nehemiah is a prime example. He received a call from God to go and rebuild the wall around Jerusalem, and instead of having a knee jerk reaction he took time to confirm what God had said and to prepare. After fasting and praying (Nehemiah 1:4), Nehemiah asked the king for permission to go and with the king's agreement, he set out for Jerusalem (Nehemiah 2:5). Upon his arrival, he didn't blurt out what God had impressed upon his heart. Instead he quietly surveyed the land, accessed the situation, and gained firsthand knowledge of the damage that had been done. Then, Nehemiah came up with a realistic plan to rebuild the wall. Following God was risky and opposition would come, but with a solid plan, Nehemiah's faith to answer God's call was strengthen by taking a calculated risk.

Sister, when you sense God is directing you to take a risk do you stop, confirm, and gather facts or do you jump right in? Faith isn't blindly following God, but rather using the good sense He gave us to be realistic and strategize a plan. It would be unwise to go to work and suddenly decide to quit because you had a revelation that this was the wrong job. It might be true and God might be tapping at your heart, but be a smart risk taker by spending time in prayer, talking with others, and looking for new opportunities. Taking risks requires faith, but we can minimize our risk when we approach it with the calculated risk strategy.

With a calculated risk mindset, faith now makes the difference between the willingness or refusal to travel unknown roads. New places can be scary. Maybe we don't understand how to navigate the uncharted territory, like what to say or to do. Without faith, it can feel impossible to imagine moving to a new city or going down a path of reestablishing a relationship with some-one who hurt you. Following God will inevitably lead to unfamiliar places and our faith will determine our readiness to go.

Abraham was called to leave his familiar home and uproot his family to travel an unknown road. The Bible says, "It was by faith that Abraham obeyed when God called him to leave home and go to another land that God would give him as his inheritance. He went without knowing where he was going" (Hebrews 11:8). Because Abraham trusted and believed God, he was willing to leave behind all that he knew in order to take hold of the promise God gave him. Faith made the difference for Abraham, and it can make the difference for you.

Is God trying to lead you to a new place, but the fear of the unknown is preventing you from going? By placing our security in worldly things like jobs, locations, or groups, we might be positioning ourselves to miss out on God's plans and purposes for our lives. But with faith, we can exchange worldly security for security in Christ. Confidence in the world will fail us, but trust in God never will. We are safer traveling the unknown roads of life with God than remaining on the known roads without God. Faith will provide the courage needed to let go of the old and walk into the new.

So, what if we have confirmed we know the path of faith God has for us and want to make a good calculated risk to follow God, yet we still get stuck? Sometimes our refusal to walk in faith is because we feel insecure or we don't like things about ourselves, or we feel like we don't have anything of value to offer God or others. It takes faith to embrace our uniqueness and believe that God calls us His masterpiece. Because we cannot see ourselves as God sees us, we can easily fall into the trap of complaining about our imperfections and comparing our differences. We cannot fathom how God can use us for His good purpose considering our weaknesses, backgrounds, and sin. Faith makes the difference between embracing ourselves or rejecting the special and unique things God put within us.

Jeremiah had doubts about his abilities. God called him to be a prophet in Judah, but Jeremiah lacked self-confidence and he didn't embrace his uniqueness. He couldn't see the workmanship of God or believe that God had set him apart as God's spokesman before he was born (Jeremiah 1:5). Jeremiah said to God, "I can't speak for you! I am too young" (Jeremiah 1:6)! But God had plans to use Jeremiah in mighty ways, and Jeremiah's fear wasn't God's roadblock. God provided where Jeremiah lacked by putting His words into Jeremiah's mouth (Jeremiah 1:9).

So often we judge ourselves and view our weaknesses as failures or as the reason why we cannot walk in courage and faith. We may try to hide our differences, and at times we may even loathe them. But faith reminds us that we are created in the image of God, and God makes no mistakes. God can use our imperfections to show His grace, love, and power in our lives. It's in our weakness that He is strong (2 Corinthians 12:9-10). Faith makes a difference in embracing our uniqueness because faith reminds us to turn away from the world and the culture, and to turn towards God to validate, define, and esteem us.

Knowing that God made each of us unique allows us to follow our God-given dreams. Faith makes the difference between pursuing our dreams or hoping they will magically happen. To pursue a God-given dream requires a steadfast faith because often following a dream means laying down other plans and ideas, or even being ridiculed by others. It might require sacrificing time or money or giving up good things that are taking the place of God's best. Believing that God set within us a plan and a purpose takes an inner strength that only God can provide.

Joseph had a dream from God, a dream that seemed out of reach after his brothers threw him into a deep hole which led to becoming a slave, and then a prison cell. However, he remained faithful to God even when it looked like his dream would not materialize. No matter what happened, Joseph put God first and he always did his best. Faith kept Joseph going until the moment his dream came true. It was a long road filled with many ups and downs. But because God was the dream Giver, He was also the dream Fulfiller.

Do you have a dream in your heart that hasn't come to fruition yet? In faith, are you actively pursuing your dreams? Like Joseph, it might not be God's timing yet, but that doesn't mean we stop pursuing. While awaiting right timing, in faith, we can take steps to prepare ourselves. Maybe we need to take a training class or strategize our finances, maybe we need to remember to put God first regardless of the completion of our dream. Whether we need to take the first step to pursuing our dreams, or wait patiently for God's timing, faith will give us the strength to take the necessary action steps to pursue and not give up.

We've *faced our fear* by focusing on Jesus, we've *stepped up to the plate of our lives* in obedience, we've prepared well by taking a *calculated risk* approach, we've reconciled *traveling unknown roads* by trusting God, we've *embraced our uniqueness* by understanding our weaknesses enhance God's power, and we've decided to *pursue our dreams* because God is the dream Giver, but we may find sometimes fear is still present. And that is okay, because we can *do it afraid*. Doing it afraid is possible with faith, and when we do it afraid we unleash the control fear has over our lives, and when we combine that with faith which unleashes the power of God, we become unstoppable. Faith and fear can exist at the same time, however, eventually faith will take over and fear will diminish. Faith is the difference maker in doing it afraid because the object of our faith, God, is so much more powerful than our fear.

The Bible says, "Yours, O LORD, is the greatness, the power, the glory, the victory, and the majesty. Everything in the heavens and on the earth is yours, O LORD, and this is your kingdom. We adore you as the one who is over all things. Wealth and honor come from you alone, for you rule over everything. Power and might are in your hand, and at your discretion people are made great and given strength" (1 Chronicles 29:11-12). With God at the center of our faith, we can conquer our fears and become courageous women of God. *Faith is the difference maker.*

ACTION STEPS:

1. Which of the four faith principles do you struggle with the most?

2. What emotion sabotages your faith the most: fear, doubt, or worry? Why?

3. Of all the *Chickening IN* pillars, which pillar is lacking the ingredient of faith?

Accepting the daily invitation from God to trust in Him, walk in faith and live courageous. Refusing to chicken out in life and instead saying "yes" to Chickening IN and the eight pillars of transformation.

Chapter 10
WILL YOU *CHICKEN IN?*

CONGRATULATIONS! SISTER, I AM SO proud of you for taking this journey with me! This book hasn't been a walk in the park because confronting
our fears, doubts, and anxieties is never easy. But we are now on this road
together along with all the other women who are committing to *Chicken IN*,
too. It takes courage to do the hard work of transformation, and *Chickening
IN* is just that: hard work. Turning from fear and walking in faith is challenging and uncomfortable, but it is also filled with hope, excitement, and the
promise that with every step of faith, God will be there to guide and lead us.

Over the span of our lives we will receive many invitations from family, friends, coworkers, church community, and even God. In fact, as I was
sitting down to write this last chapter I got an invitation from my husband
to go on a family bike ride. We live in a small mountain town that is well
known for having outdoor trails for cycling, hiking, and riding. Since we are
not experienced mountain bikers, my husband recommended that we return
to a familiar trail, and I agreed. We quickly got our gear on and headed out
the door for a fun afternoon. However, what I thought would be a leisurely
bike ride quickly turned into a *Chickening IN* moment, or, should I confess,
a chickening out moment! The trail that was familiar to us was not exactly
how we remembered it. This time, the hills were steeper and the terrain was
more uneven and filled with ruts that previously went unnoticed. Probably
because in the past we had ridden this road on our gas powered, four-wheel

quads—vehicles that were built to endure the rough ground. But we had never attempted it on our mountain bikes, and from the view of my pedals it was down-right scary.

As I gazed at the first incline of the trail, I received another invitation. This invite didn't come from my husband or my daughter, but from fear. Fear was asking me to walk away and quit. The voice of fear was strong, and relentlessly it attacked my thoughts. It's like back in high school when my best friend begged me to go to the "biggest, most important party" of our senior year. I wanted to say no, but instead I entertained the idea, and after thinking about it too long I ended up RSVPing with a *yes* by default. There I was at the bottom of the hill, the woman writing the final chapter of *Chickening IN,* and I was listening to my fear instead of facing it.

My husband and daughter reached the top of the first hill and they shouted words of encouragement. But I was too busy lingering in fear where it was noisy, not with the loud music of a party, but with worries and doubts about falling off my bike or not having enough strength to make it up the hill. My husband descended down and pulled up right behind me. Another invitation came. He offered to walk up the mountain right next to me, and if I fell he would catch me. I was terrified, but I had a choice to make: stay with fear and let it control me, or say *yes* to my husband and conquer this thing. Still scared, I surveyed the pathway to determine the best side to ride on. Then, I faced fear by deciding to *Chicken IN* and do it afraid, and when my fear and I reached the top of the hill, my fear shrunk back and my courage got stronger.

That day I was reminded that fear is a battle mostly played out in the circumference of my mind. Rarely is it ever about a physical roaring lion or tangible burning flames. Instead, fear invites me to engage in doubtful and worrisome thoughts that try to hold me back from pursuing good things like a necessary and needed change or following my dreams. Fear starts pinging my mind with, *what-if you fail, what-if you can't, what-if you get hurt.* But fear doesn't disclose that ninety-nine percent of the time the what-if's never come true. And every time we accept the invitation to be fearful we position ourselves to believe in an outcome that may never come to pass.

I was reminded that day that we need to ask God to renew our courage daily. Life is too unpredictable, dynamic, and fluid. Often, we are caught off guard because circumstances can change on a dime. Just when we think we've mastered our fears we will be confronted with a new situation that requires new courage. That is why *Chickening IN* is not a one-time invitation and magically all your fears are gone. No, that would be unrealistic. Rather it's an offer to embrace a daily mindset of courage and faith, it's a lifestyle of refusing to let fear win, and it's developing a resistance to the feelings of fear, worry, and doubt.

I am so honored that you accepted the invitation in chapter one to read this book. The decision to become a fearless woman of God is made much easier with the practical steps offered within each pillar. But the road doesn't end here—rather the opposite—it just begins. *Chickening IN* is not a "one and done" or a quick fix formula to a fear-free life. It's an invitation to choose faith over fear every day, and the principles laid out within the eight pillars of *Chickening IN* are the foundation to build a courageous life upon. They are like a guidepost directing us away from fearfulness and pointing us toward a new brave approach to life. It is a process of becoming, and accepting this invitation is a *daily* decision to lay down fear and take up courage.

If you accept this invitation you are embarking into the land of transformation. A place where fear-filled lives can be reconstructed into courageous faith-filled lives. This is how God is transforming me from the inside out, and every pillar of *Chickening IN* is a tool in God's hands to restore my life. However, I've learned that I must be willing to act in faith by moving regardless of how I feel. God extends a daily invitation to trust Him and believe that what He says is true, but it's up to me to accept. Every day I have to RSVP by saying *yes*. God's invitation has your name written on it, too! He is offering you a new life where you can break free from the prison of fear, doubt, and

worry. A life filled with adventure, hope, meaning, and purpose. Have you responded to Him
with a *yes?*

over and over God
invites us to have
courageous faith.

Over and over God invites us to have coura-
geous faith. In fact, there are more than 300 Bible verses commanding us to
fear not, don't be afraid, or to have courage. Christine Caine says in her book
Undaunted, "He knew that we would be afraid, that we would doubt. That's
why He tells us again and again in the Bible, 'Fear not.'"[18] Maybe that's why
God dedicates a chunk of Scripture to encouraging us to be brave—He knew
we would need reassurance and support not just once, but on an ongoing
basis. However, in order to be strengthened by God's Word we have to know
it. We must study and learn the Scriptures to become the courageous and
fearless women we desire to be. These ten Bible verses are my favorite courage
verses, and they have been instrumental in boosting my courage so I could
take leaps of faith I never thought possible. I recommend compiling a list of
your own, or if you want you can use my list:

"This is my command—be strong and courageous! Do not be afraid
or discouraged. For the LORD your God is with you wherever you
go" (Joshua 1:9).

"Wait patiently for the LORD. Be brave and courageous. Yes, wait
patiently for the LORD" (Psalm 27:14).

"So be strong and courageous, all you who put your hope in the
LORD" (Psalm 31:24)!

"Don't call everything a conspiracy, like they do, and don't live
in dread of what frightens them. Make the LORD of Heaven's
Armies holy in your life. He is the one you should fear. He is the
one who should make you tremble" (Isaiah 8:12-13).

"Don't be afraid, for I am with you. Don't be discouraged, for I am
your God. I will strengthen you and help you. I will hold you up
with my victorious right hand" (Isaiah 41:10).

"But now, O Jacob, listen to the LORD who created you. O Israel, the one who formed you says, 'Do not be afraid, for I have ransomed you. I have called you by name; you are mine. When you go through deep waters, I will be with you. When you go through rivers of difficulty, you will not drown. When you walk through the fire of oppression, you will not be burned up; the flames will not consume you" (Isaiah 43:1-2).

"Your road led through the sea, your pathway through the mighty waters—a pathway no one knew was there" (Psalm 77:19)!

"As soon as I pray, you answer me; you encourage me by giving me strength" (Psalm 138:3).

"Do not be afraid or discouraged, for the LORD will personally go ahead of you. He will be with you; he will neither fail you nor abandon you" (Deuteronomy 31:8).

"For God has not given us a spirit of fear and timidity, but of power, love, and self-discipline" (2 Timothy 1:7).

Sister, I like to keep things real. Transformation is a process, and our perfect, fear-free selves are not on this side of Heaven. However, we can make progress and maybe even take huge leaps. But I'd like to encourage you to be patient. More often I have seen God's transformation in my life take place in the small steps of faith.

If it were possible to see you face-to-face, during our visit I'd want to hear your story and learn about the fears and doubts that have held you hostage. I'd ask you, "What things happened in your past that caused you to not trust in anyone, including God? What childhood pain and brokenness are you still carrying and what lies do you believe about yourself that might be keeping you from being brave and courageous? Is fear preventing you from walking in faith?"

Then, I would share my story, too, because I am a broken woman just like you. I'd tell you about my struggle with fear, worry, and anxiety, and maybe I'd show you my feet, because they bear calluses that reflect the hard road of

pain and brokenness I have endured. I would also let
you know about the restoration that is occurring in
my life. I am not who I used to be! I am transform-

will you *chicken
IN* with me?

ing into the woman who God is calling me to be. No longer am I bound by the
stronghold of fear because God is changing me. Each pillar of *Chickening IN* is
how He is doing it, and I would offer these tools to you, too!

Before our visit is over, I'm sure we'd shed a few tears over our past brokenness, our mistakes, and the lack of trust in God we've had, and then we'd
giggle together because of the insanity of it all. We'd both agree that having
faith and boldly trusting God is the answer, but wholeheartedly trusting in
what we cannot see is difficult. Then, we'd encourage each other to turn from
our fears, and to accept Christ's invitation to cast our burdens upon Him
(Matthew 11:29). Yoking ourselves with Christ is what we need to lighten the
load of *Chickening IN*. Both of us would acknowledge that our victory to overcome must come from God's power and not our own. When it was time to say
goodbye, we'd embrace in a sister hug that would say, "I am here for you, and
I am on your side. You are not alone on this journey, because I will walk by
your side." What a precious time it would be!

And what a precious time it was when my six-year-old daughter first invited me to *Chicken IN*. It was a silly phrase spoken by a child that propelled
me to make bold decisions to face my fears and walk in faith. Sometimes a
single word or phrase has the power to change the course of our lives, and
Chickening IN is that word for me. That is how God is transforming my life
from the inside out. Like the flip of a switch, *Chickening IN* created an epiphany or a God moment. Where there was hopelessness, fear, and doubt, now
there is newfound hope, courage, and strength. It was exactly what I needed
to get my feet moving and my faith growing.

Sister, how lovely it would be to sip tea together. Though we can't be
in person we can still travel this *Chickening IN* journey together in spirit, in
prayer, and in unity with Christ. Do you want to take hold of the amazing,

adventurous, and fearless life God has planned for you? Will you RSVP with a *yes* to my invitation to join me as we conquer our fears, defeat our worries, and transform our fears to courageous faith? Will you *Chicken IN* with me? I can't wait for what Christ is going to do in and through you!

ENDNOTES

1 "What Is Faith?" Focus on the Family, November 10, 2019. https://www.focusonthefamily.com/parenting/what-is-faith/. (Accessed 2/01/2020).

2 Stinkin Thinkin. Joyce Meyer Ministries, 2018. https://www.facebook.com/watch/?v=10156615639022384. (Accessed 2/01/2020).

3 Warren, Rick. The Purpose Driven Life: What on Earth Am I Here For?. Grand Rapids, MI: Zondervan, 2002. p. 29.

4 Lucado, Max. *Fearless Small Group Discussion Guide*. Nashville: Thomas Nelson Publishing, 2009, 26.

5 Ortberg, John. *All The Places to Go . . . How Will you Know?: God Has Placed before You an Open Door. What Will You Do?*. Carol Stream: Tyndale Publishers, Inc., 2015, 15.

6 I heard this quote in a sermon podcast, but I do not recall which one to give due credit.

7 Ibid, 13.

8 Ibid, 39.

9 Ibid, 91.

10 Shirer, Priscilla. *Fervent: A Woman's Battle Plan for Serious, Specific, and Strategic Prayer*. Narrated by Priscilla Shirer. Nashville: B&H Publishing Group, 2015. Audiobook.

11 Unice, Nicole. *She's Got Issues: Seriously Good News for Stressed-Out, Secretly Scared Control Freaks Like Us.* Carol Stream: Tyndale Publishers, Inc., 2012, 118.

12 Ortberg, John. *All The Places to Go . . . How Will you Know?: God Has Placed before You an Open Door. What Will You Do?.* Carol Stream: Tyndale Publishers, Inc., 2015, 97.

13 Warren, Rick. "God's Dream for Your Life." *Daily Hope,* September 2017, https://pastorrick.com/archive/.

14 Parks, Rosa and Reed, Gregory J. *Quiet Strength: The Faith, the Hope, and the Heart of a Woman Who Changed a Nation.* Grand Rapids: Zondervan Publishing House, 1994, 17.

15 Ortberg, John. *All The Places to Go . . . How Will you Know?: God Has Placed before You an Open Door. What Will You Do?.* Carol Stream: Tyndale Publishers, Inc., 2015, 28.

16 Young, Sarah. *Jesus Calling: Enjoying Peace in His Presence.* Nashville: Thomas Nelson, Inc., 2004, 178.

17 Ortberg, John. *All The Places to Go, . . . How Will you Know?: God Has Placed before You an Open Door. What Will You Do?.* Carol Stream: Tyndale Publishers, Inc., 2015, 84.

18 Caine, Christine. *Undaunted: Daring to Do What God Calls You to Do.* Grand Rapids: Zondervan Publishing House, 2012, 113.

JJ GUTIERREZ

JJ Gutierrez is living the *Chickening IN* life! She didn't start out as a courageous, brave woman of God. Growing up in a home where her mother had multiple marriages and then her mother's death when JJ was just eighteen years old had a profound effect on her need for security and certainty. Fear and anxiety planted deep seeds that carried into her young adulthood . . . seeds that grew into a fearful lifestyle. Becoming a Christian in her early twenties started the transformation process, but it would take years of confronting fears and learning to trust God before God's truth grew bigger than her fear. Her firsthand knowledge in overcoming fear makes her well equipped to share her *Chickening IN* journey. JJ has made some very bold and courageous decisions including quitting her six-figure income career and becoming a homeschool mom. She attributes any success or victories over fear to her twenty-five year relationship with Jesus Christ. JJ lives in Southern California with her husband and tween daughter. Her two oldest daughters have launched into adulthood.

For more information about

JJ Gutierrez
and
Chickening IN
please connect at:

www.chickeningin.com
jj@chickeningin.com
www.facebook.com/chickeningin
@ChickeningIN
www.instagram.com/chickening_in

For more information about
AMBASSADOR INTERNATIONAL
please connect at:

www.ambassador-international.com
@AmbassadorIntl
www.facebook.com/AmbassadorIntl

*If you enjoyed this book, please consider leaving us a review on
Amazon, Goodreads, or our website.*

More from Ambassador International

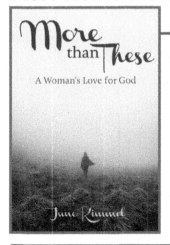

More Than These addresses the question that every woman who desires to walk with God must face: How can a woman love God as she should and keep the rest of her life in its proper place? Women are searching for the secret to balancing their lives. More Than These: A Woman's Love for God declares that loving God supremely is the answer.

More Than These
by June Kimmel

Could it be women are so busy chasing emptiness and playing the people-pleasing game, that they can't find time to live on mission? It's time to take a deep breath and do some inventory, to dig in and see what God's Word has to say about this tug-of-war between our flesh and our mission, and to figure out ways to quit chasing emptiness and take bold steps of obedience. What would happen if we said Enough of Me . . . more Jesus?

Enough of Me

by Priscilla Peters

Using her own personal journey during an adventurous move to Paris, Anne shares healing truths of Scripture and methods she found to help others find freedom from their baggage. You will be inspired and refreshed as you realize you no longer have to carry your baggage either.

Pack Your Baggage, Honey, We're Moving to Paris!

by Anne Farnum